AF473982

NORMAN ACKROYD A SHETLAND NOTEBOOK

Royal Academy of Arts

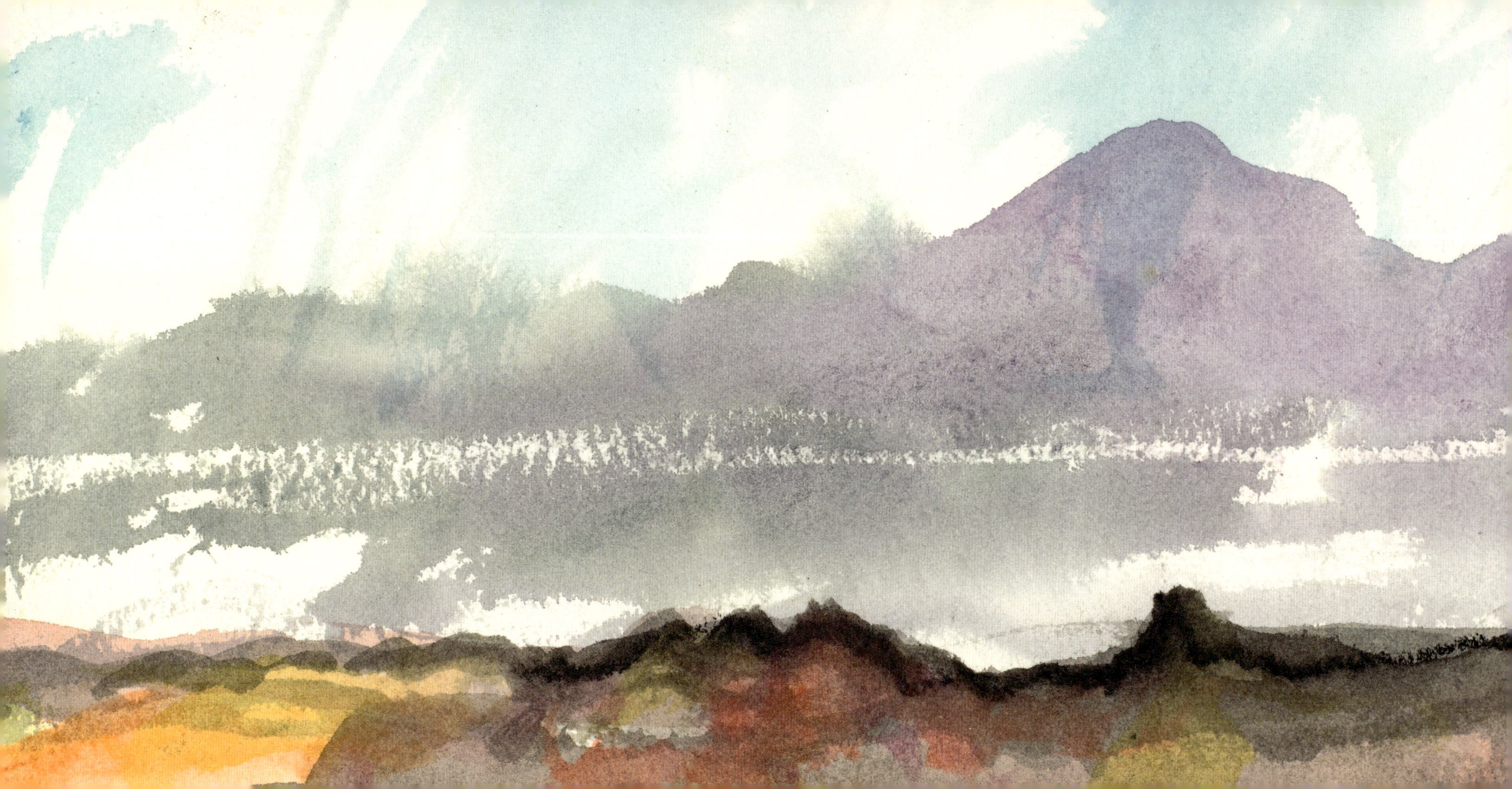

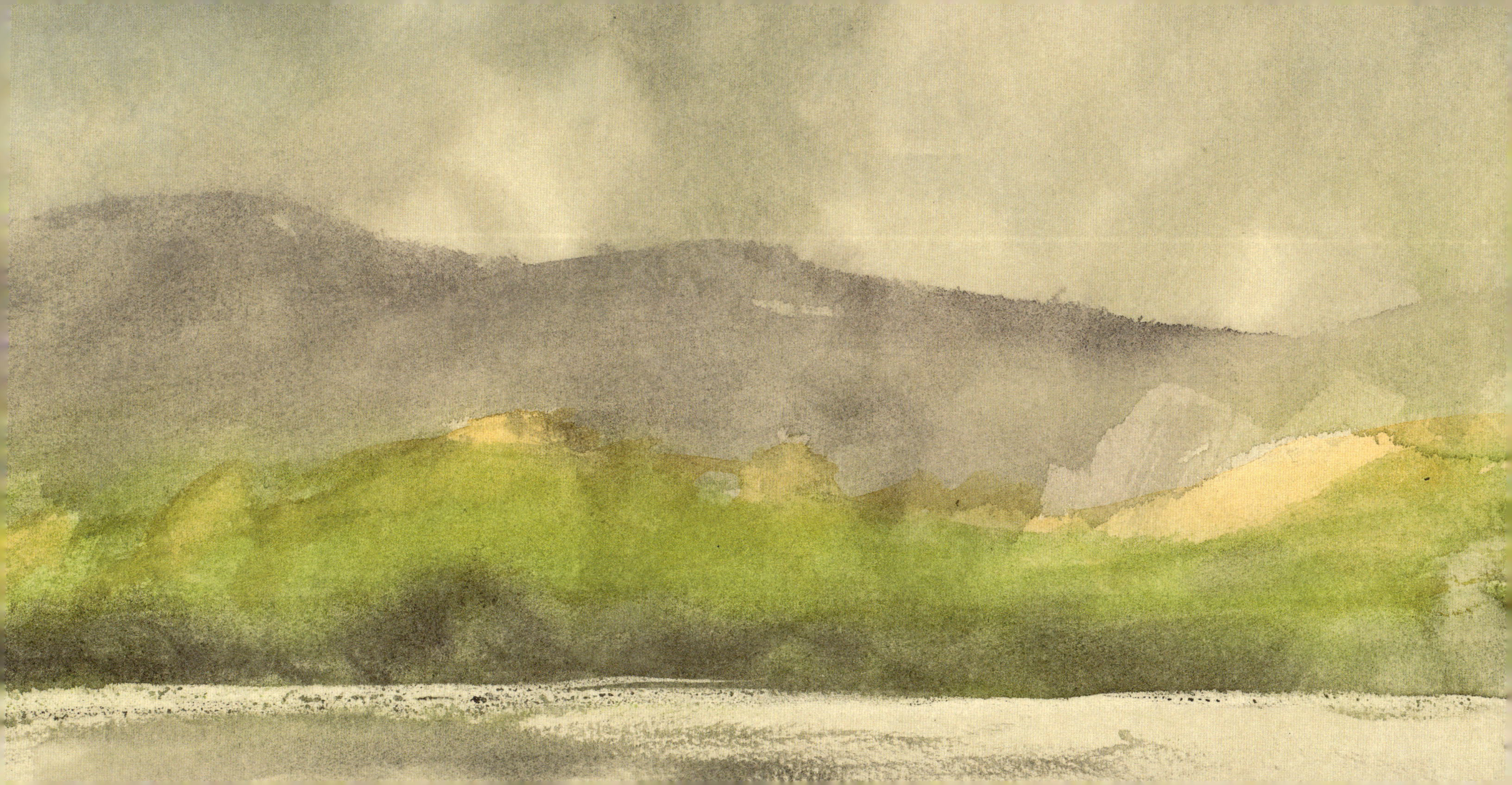

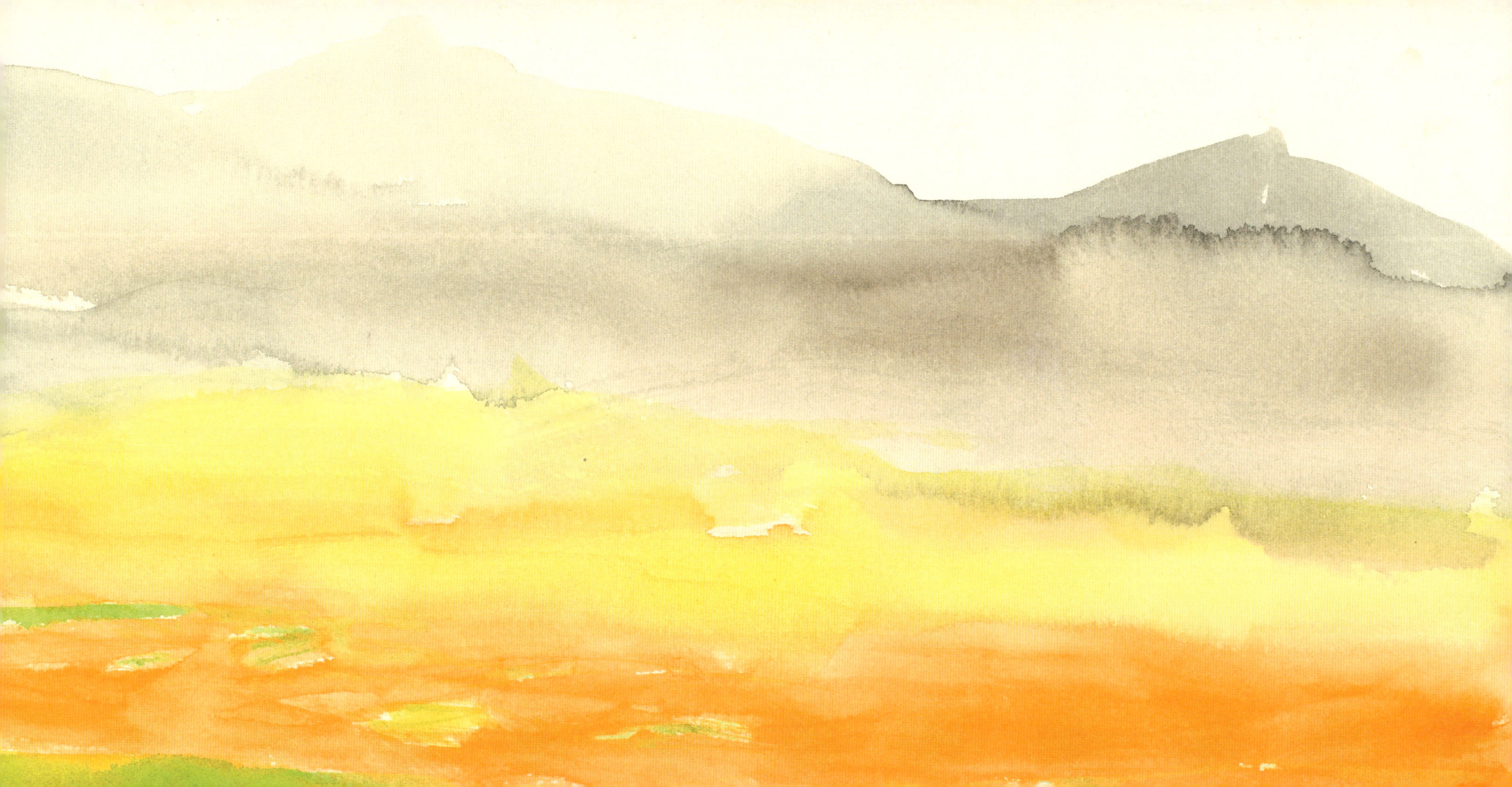

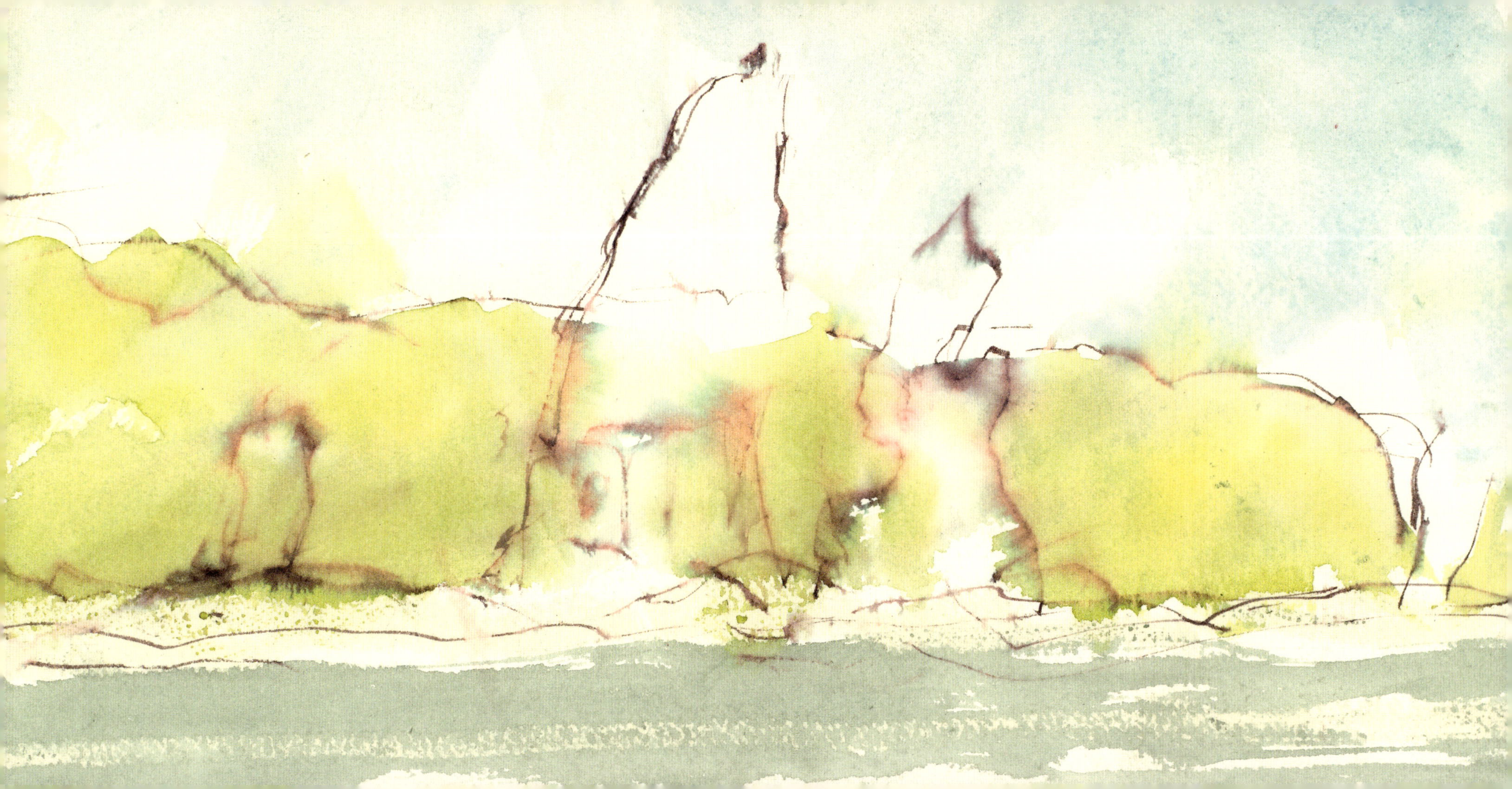

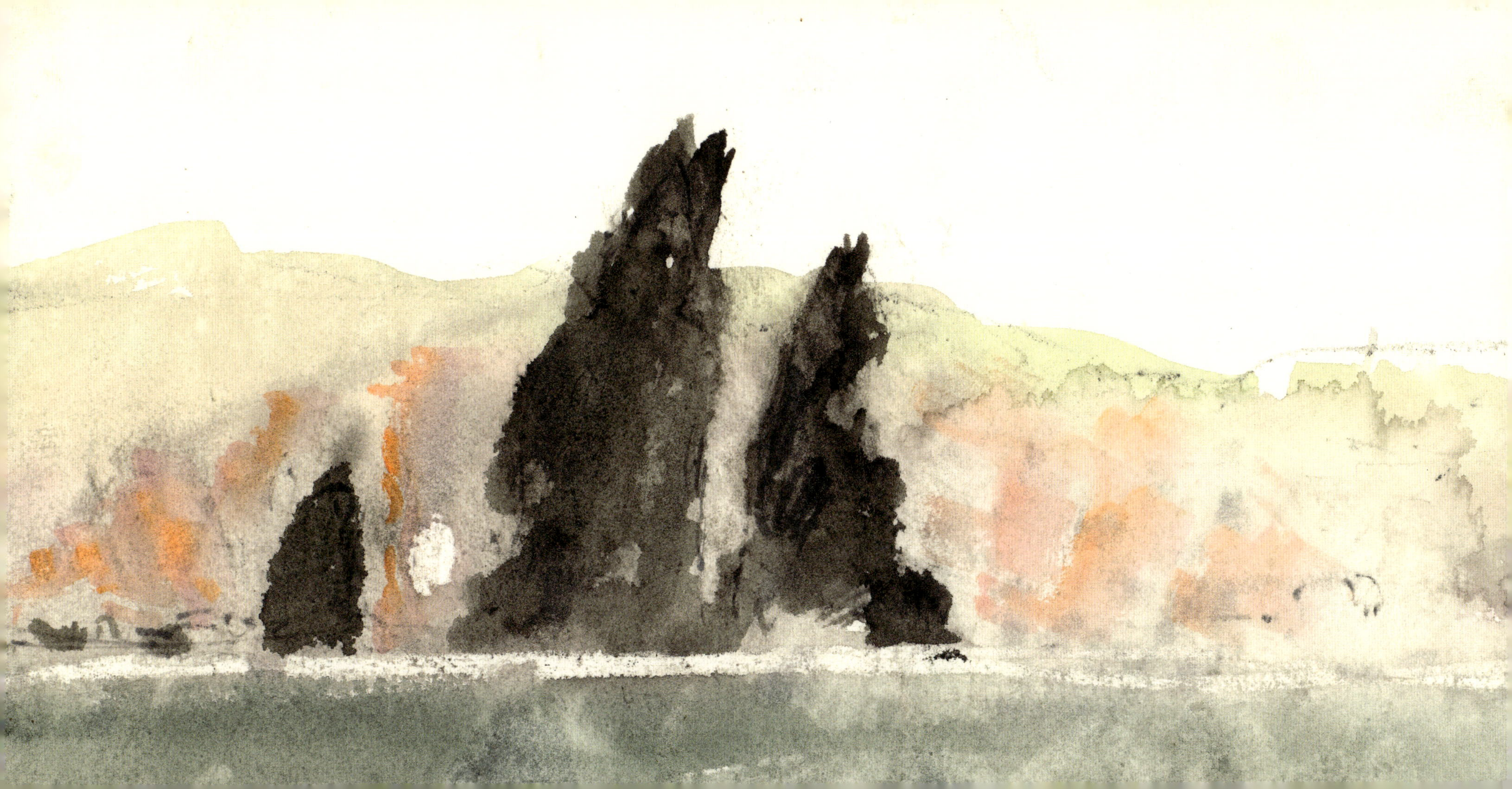

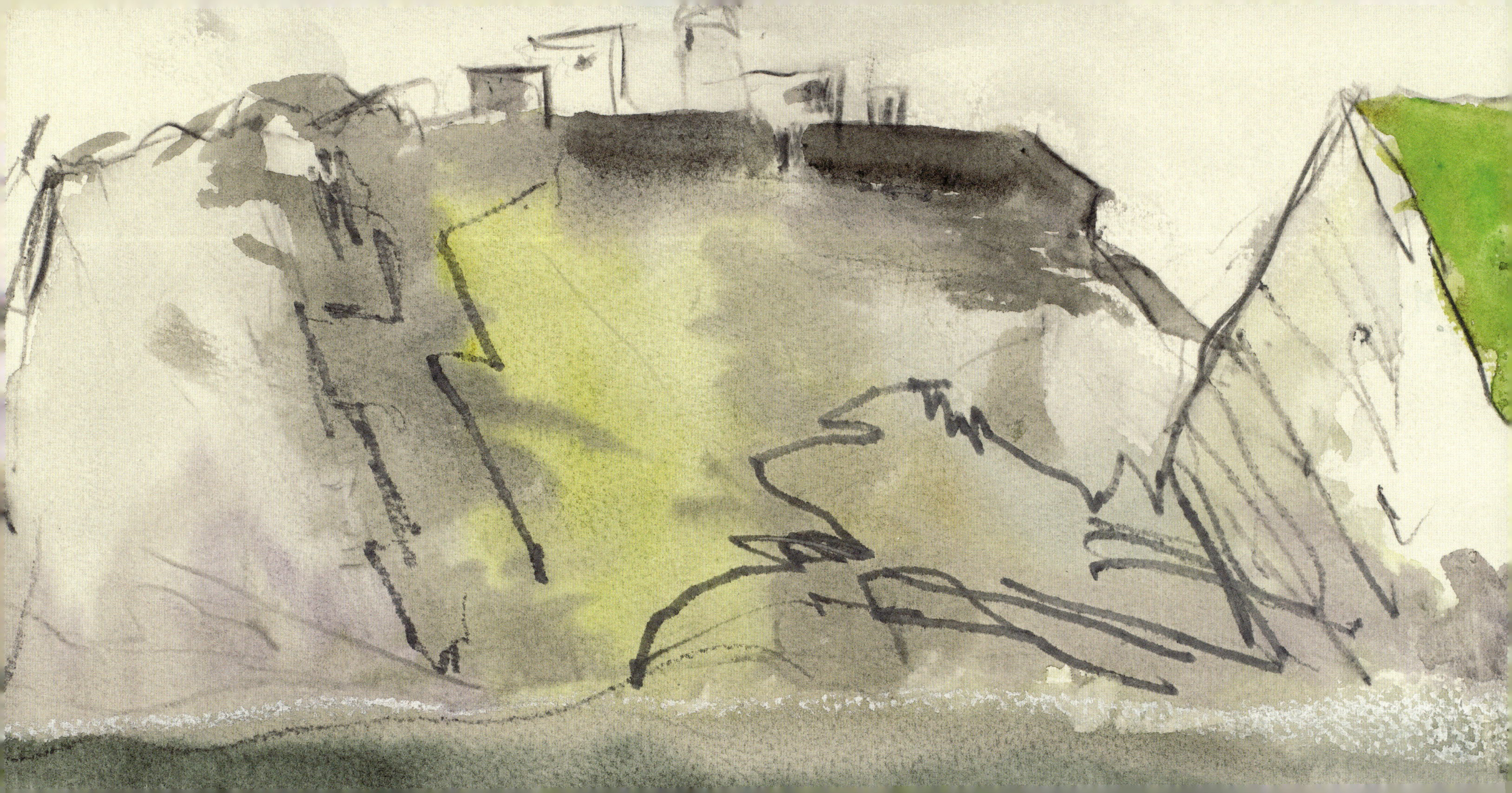

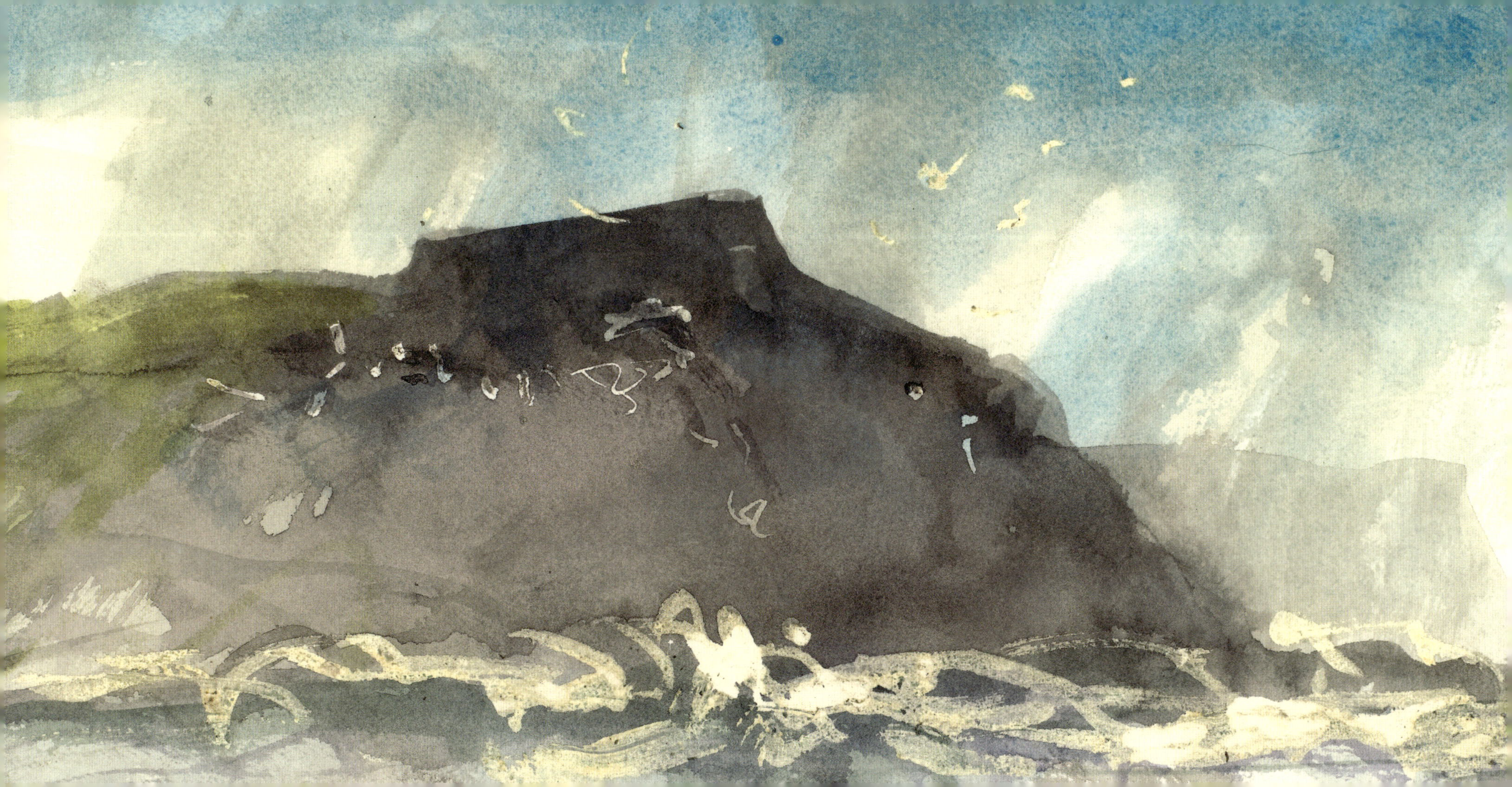

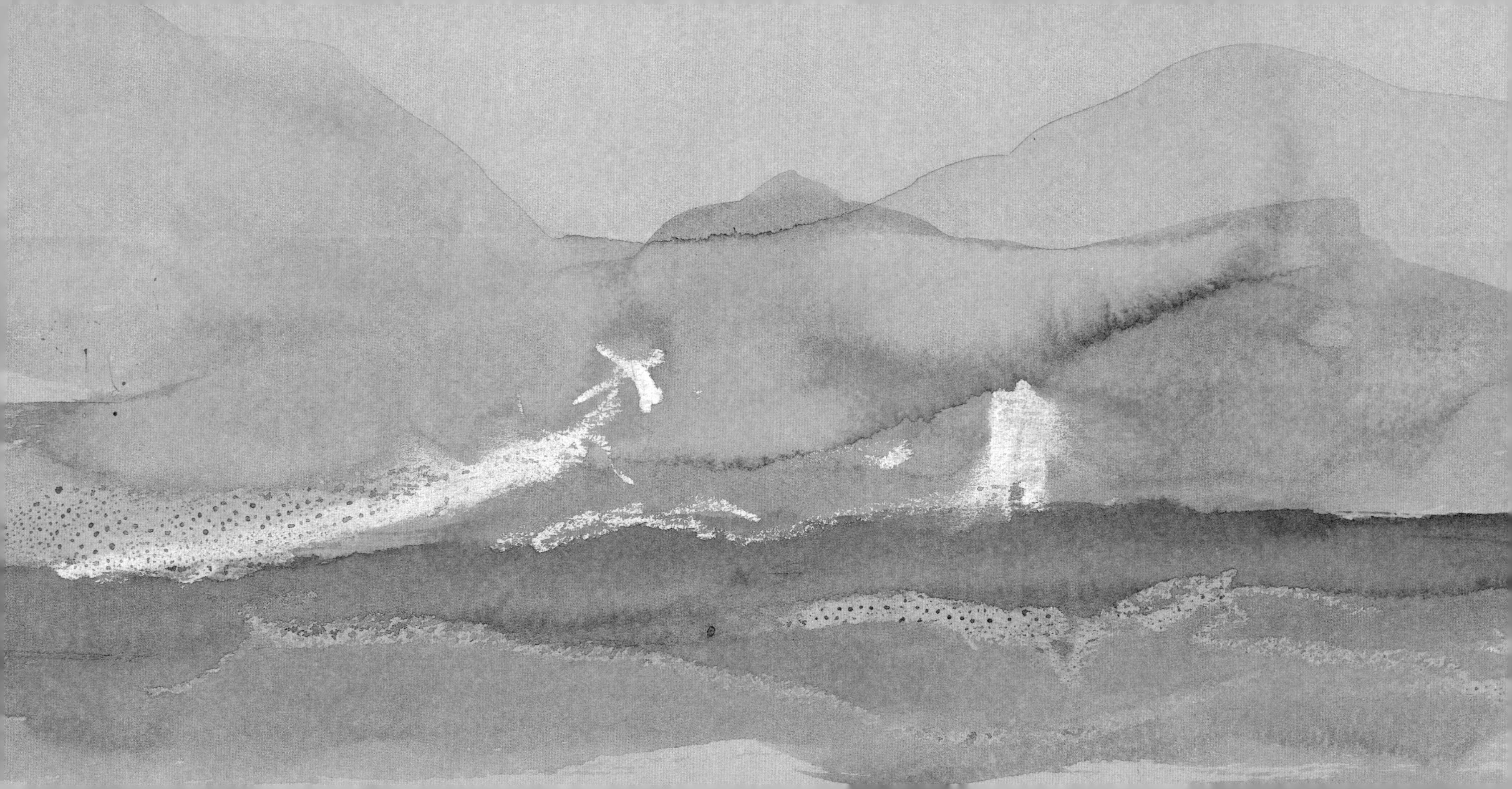

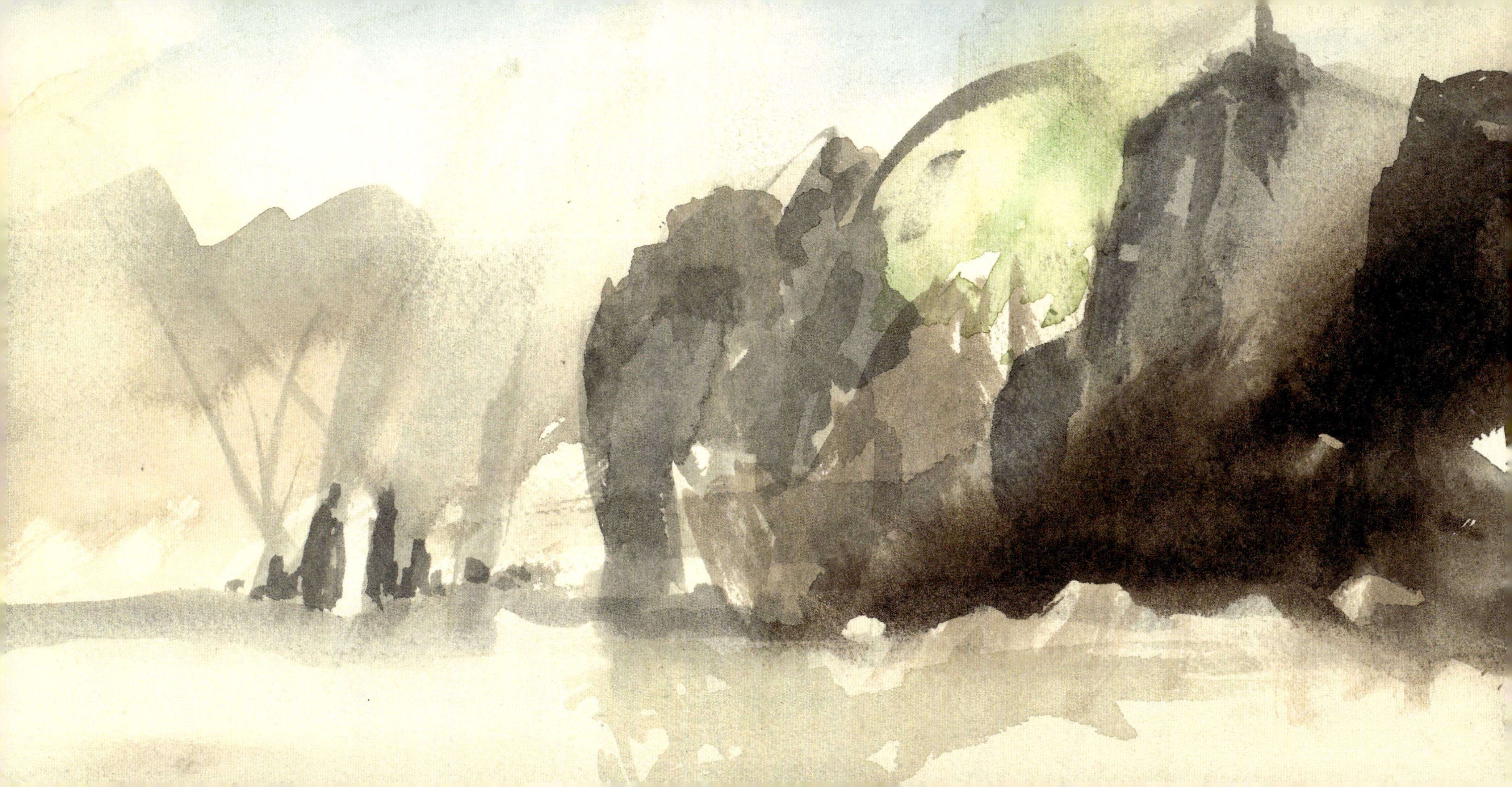

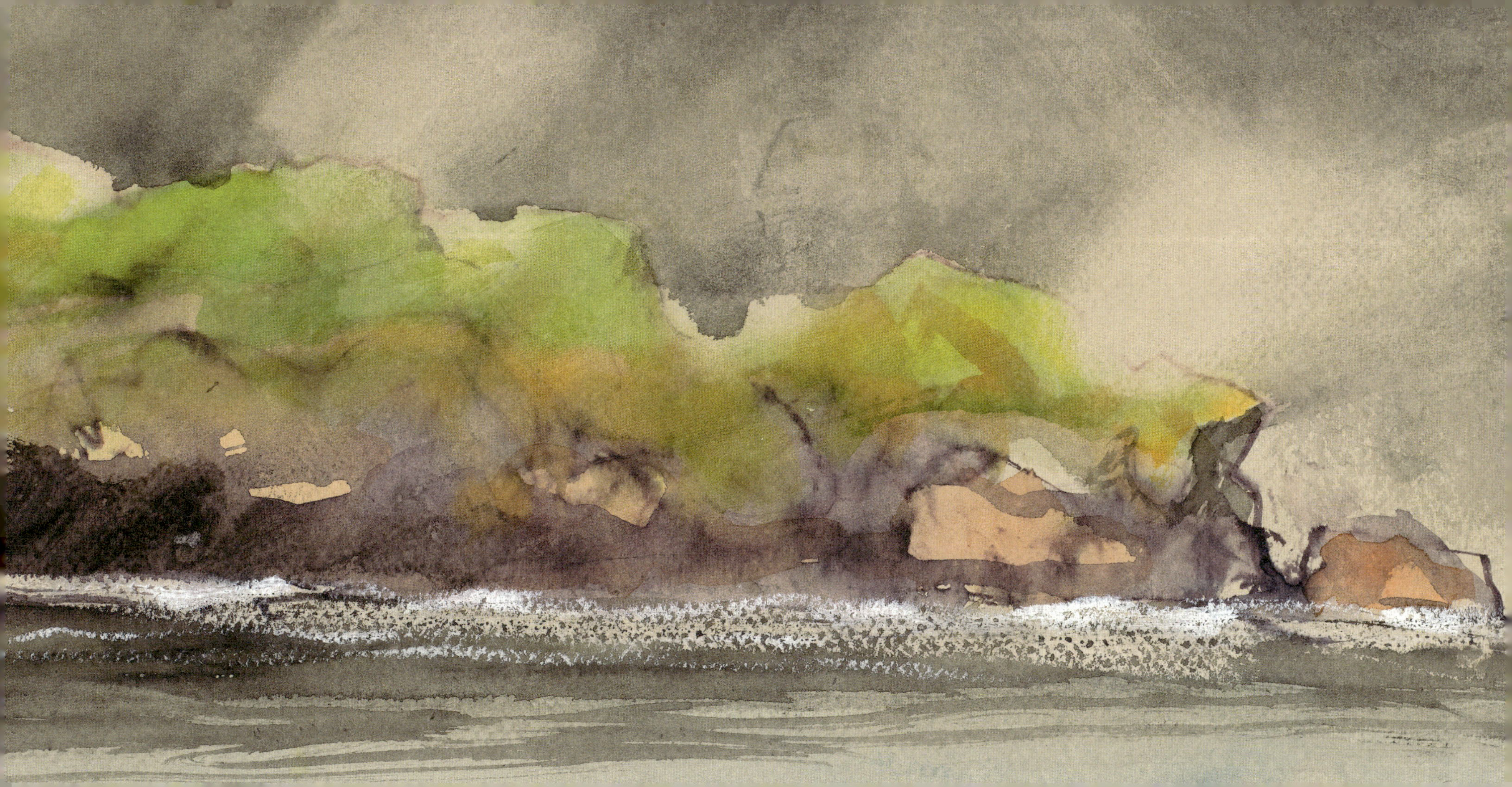

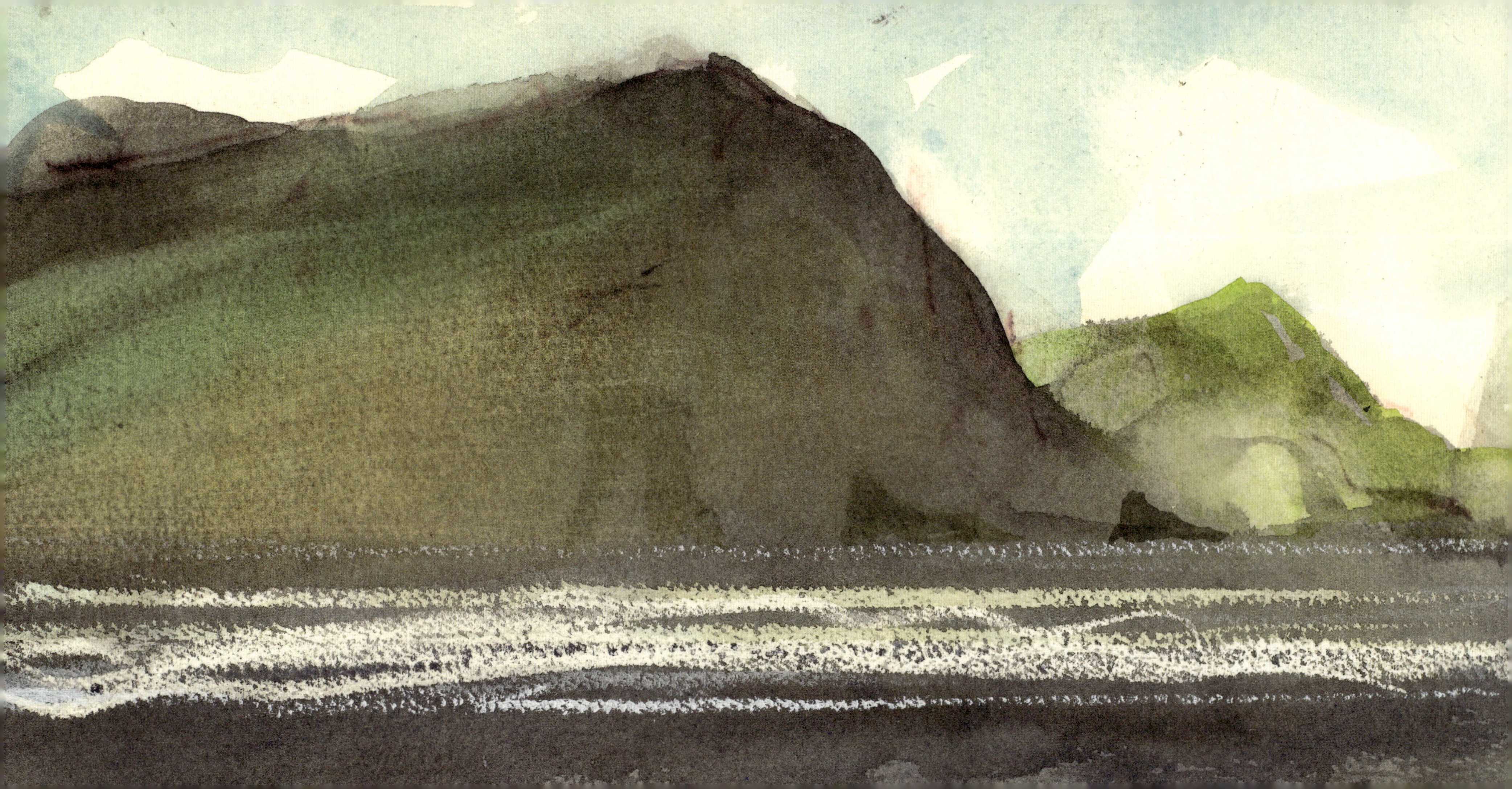

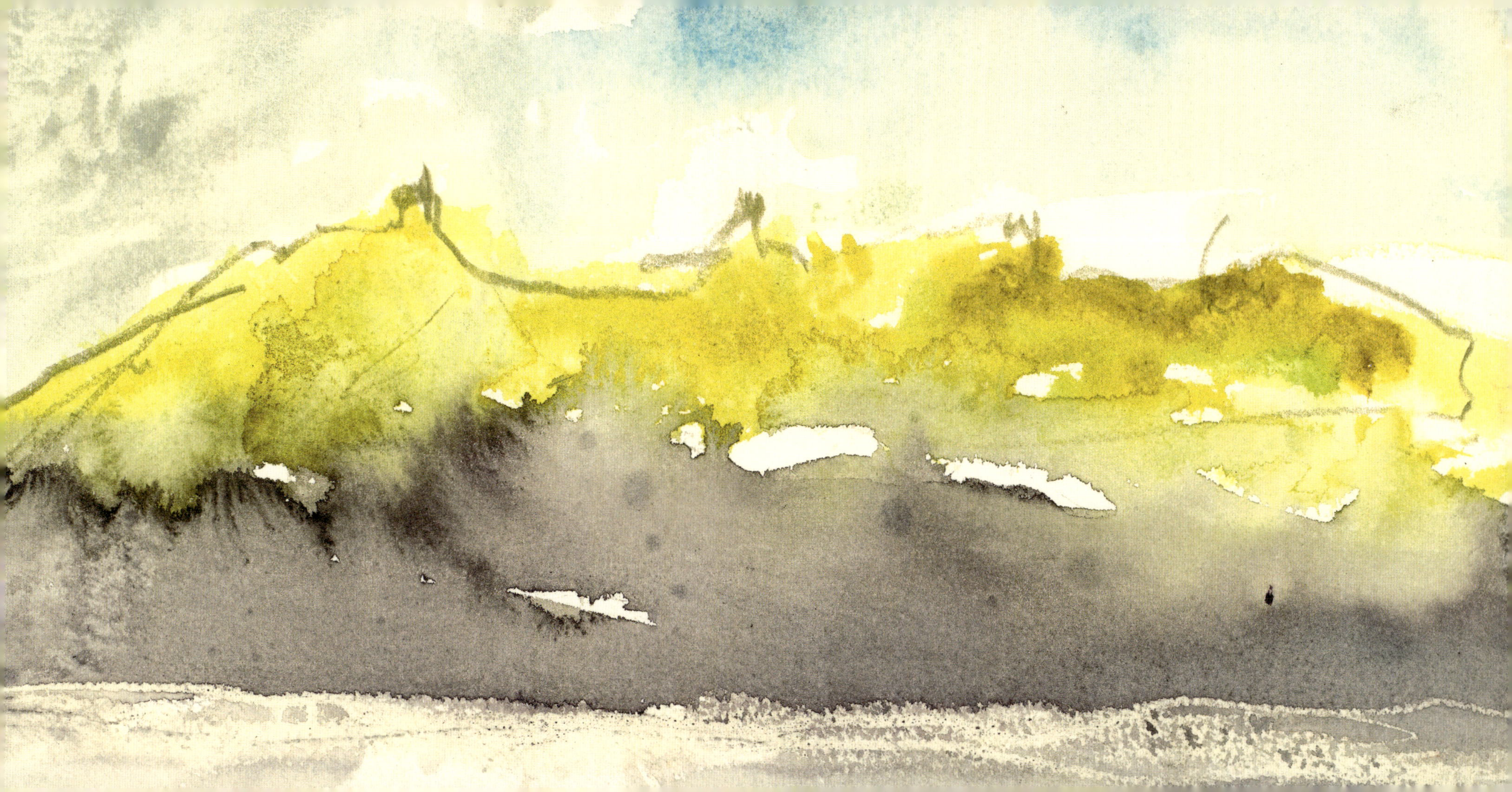

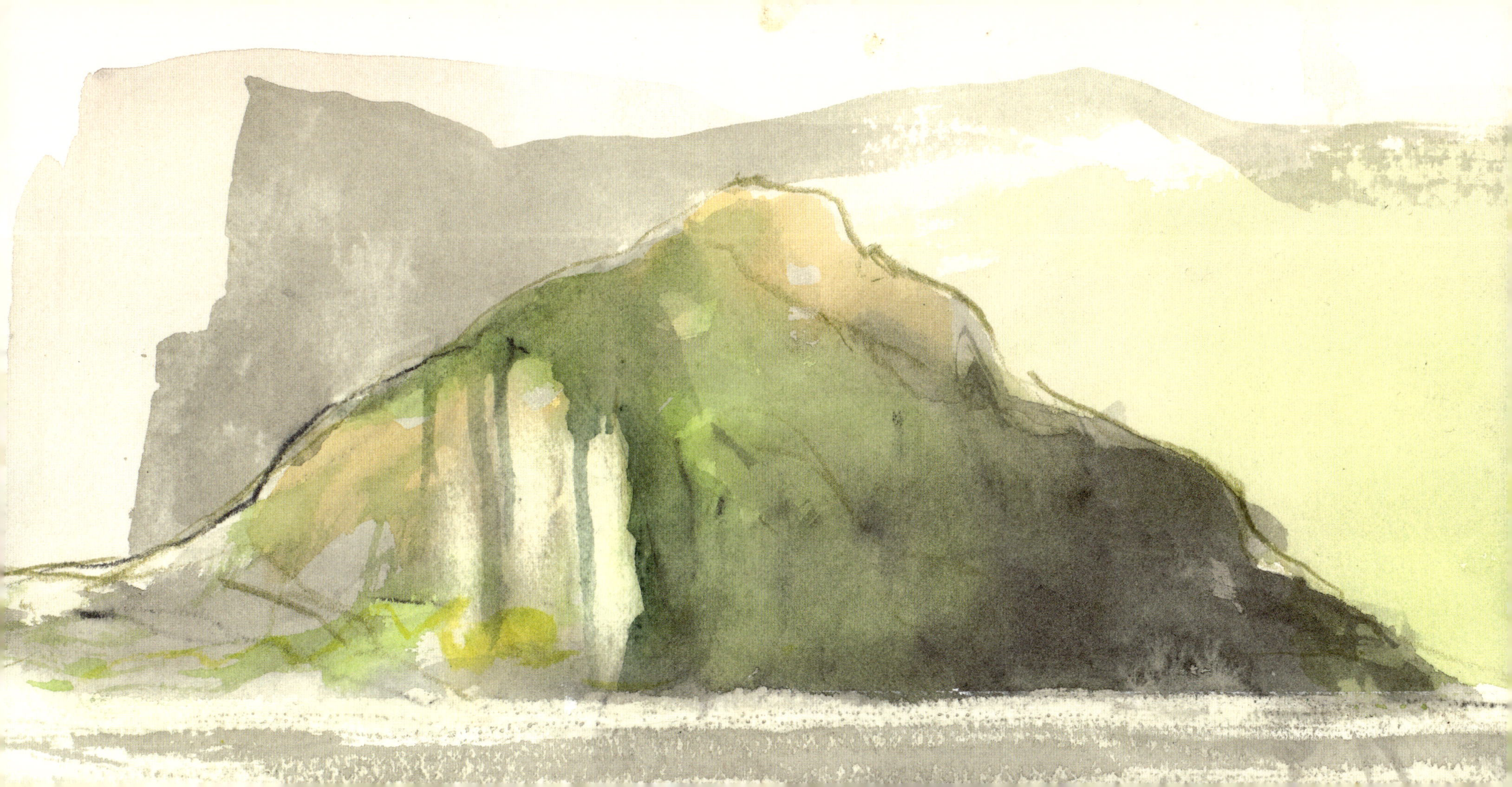

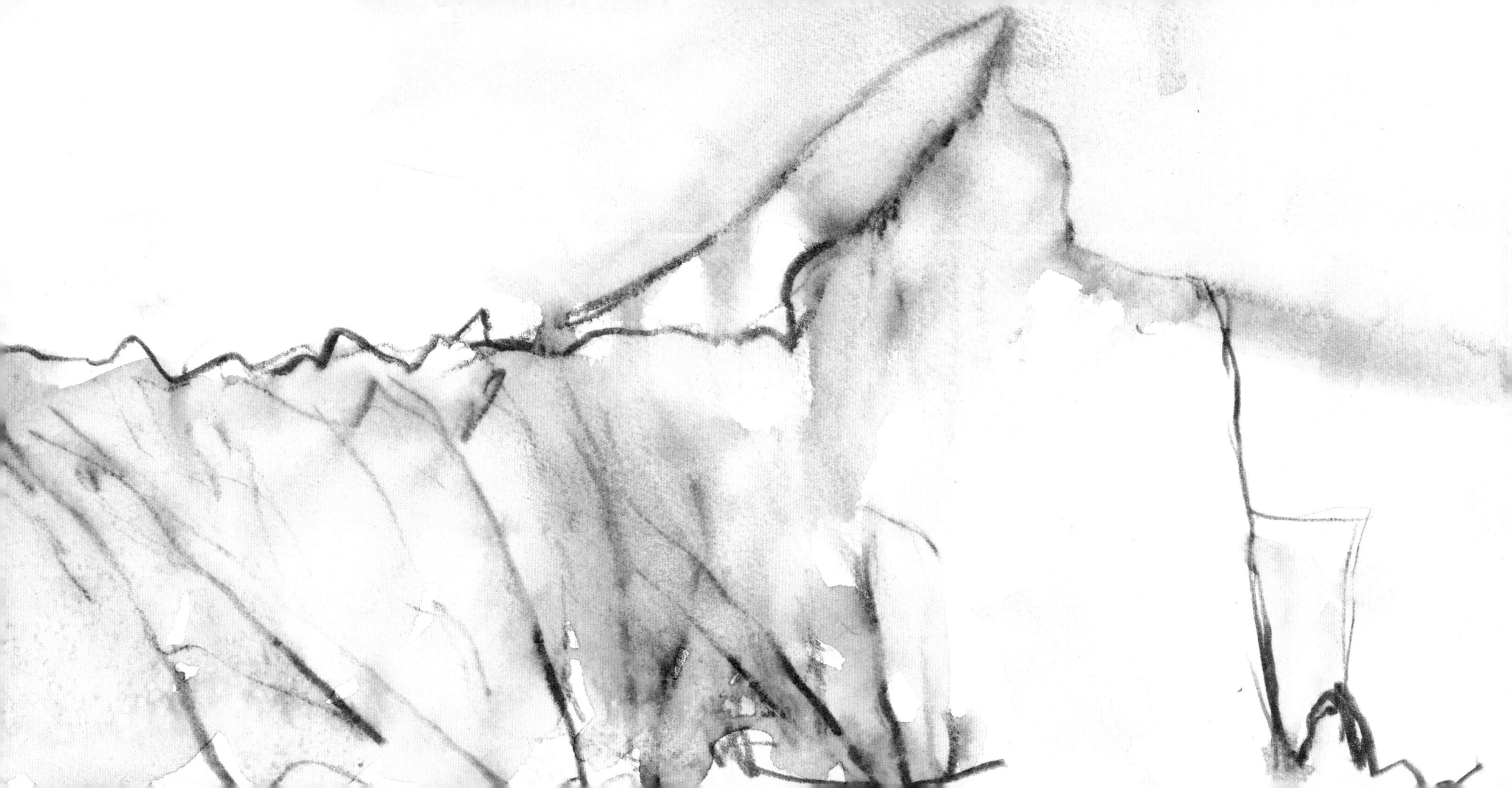

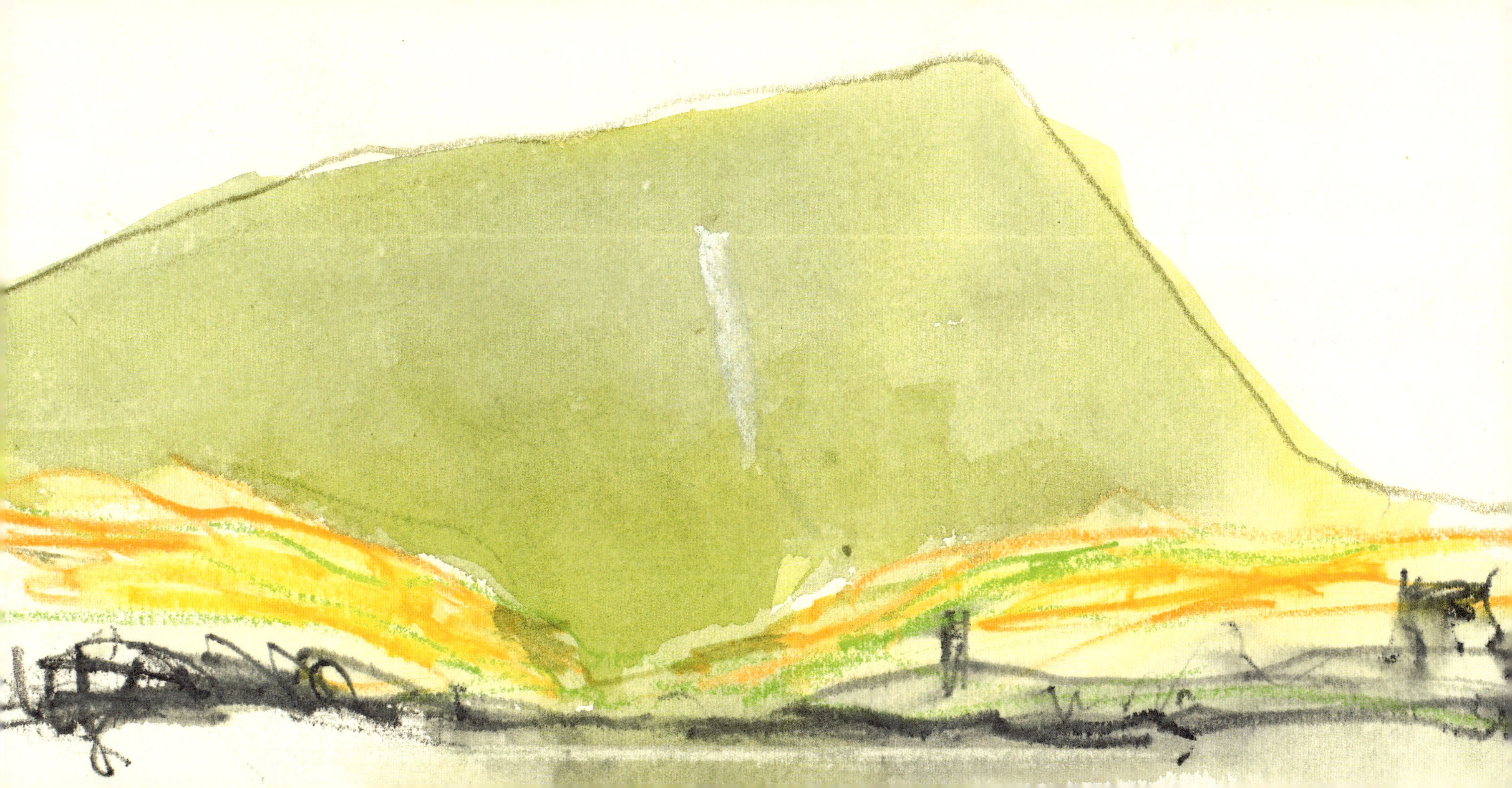

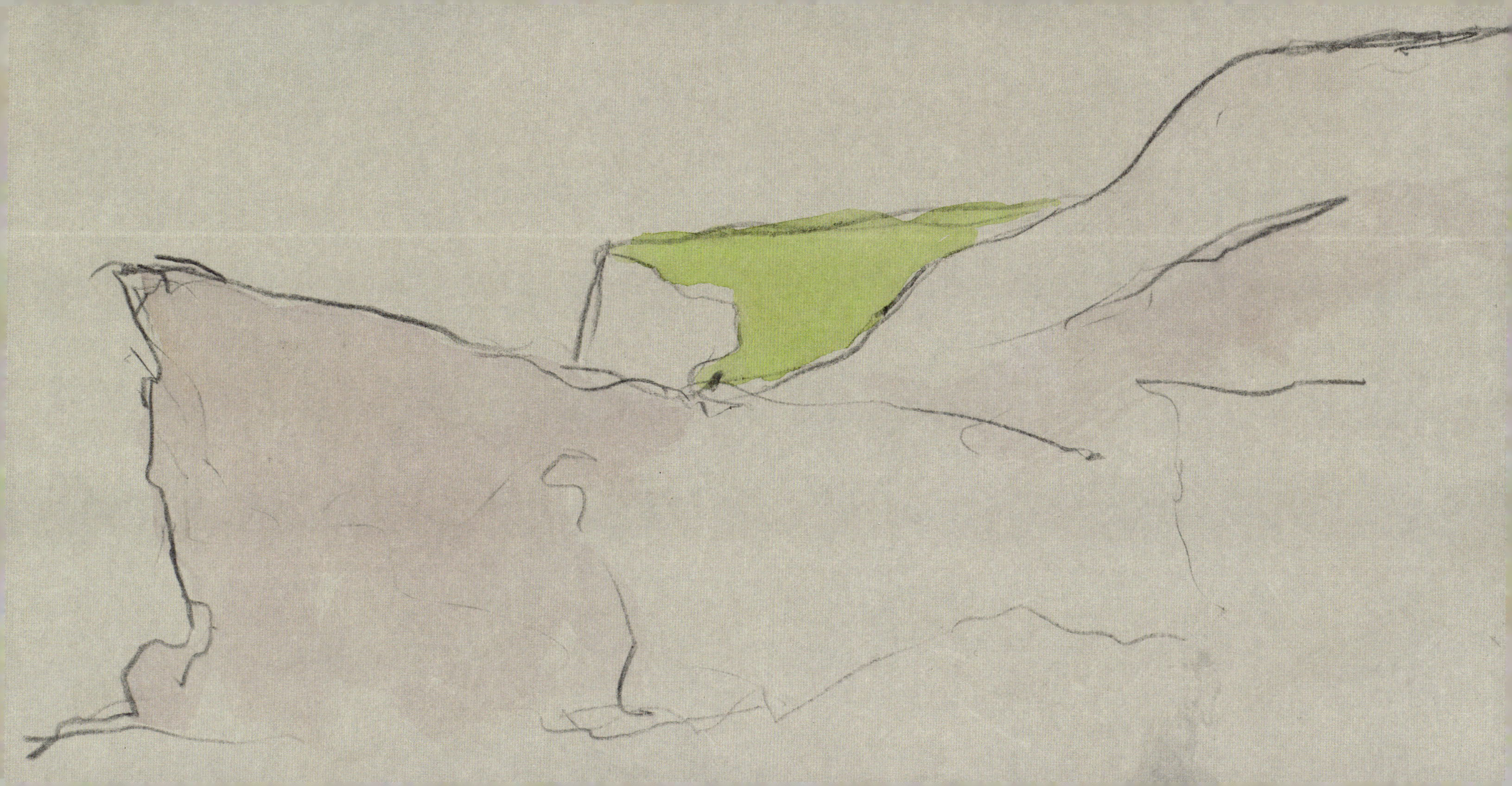

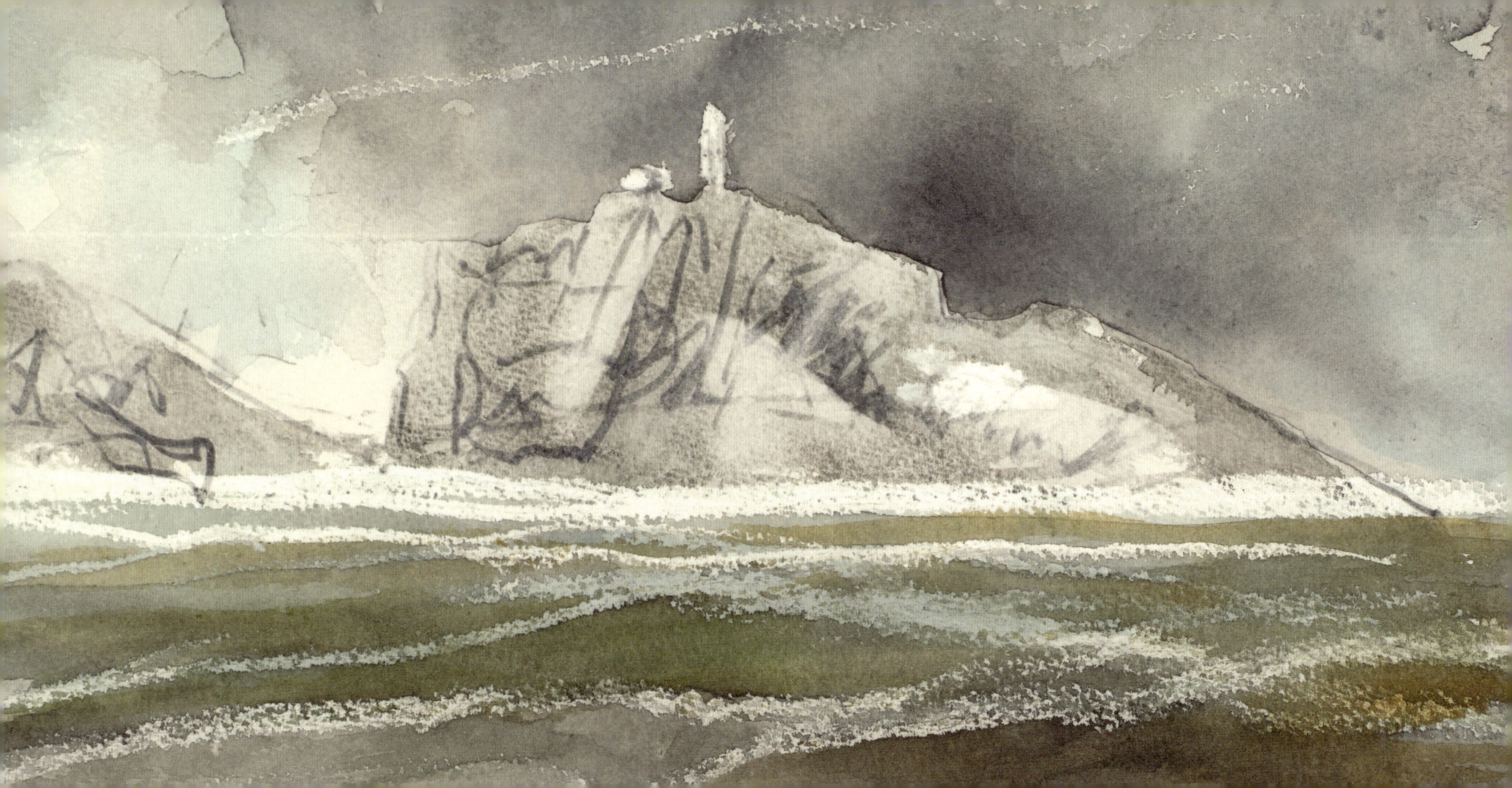

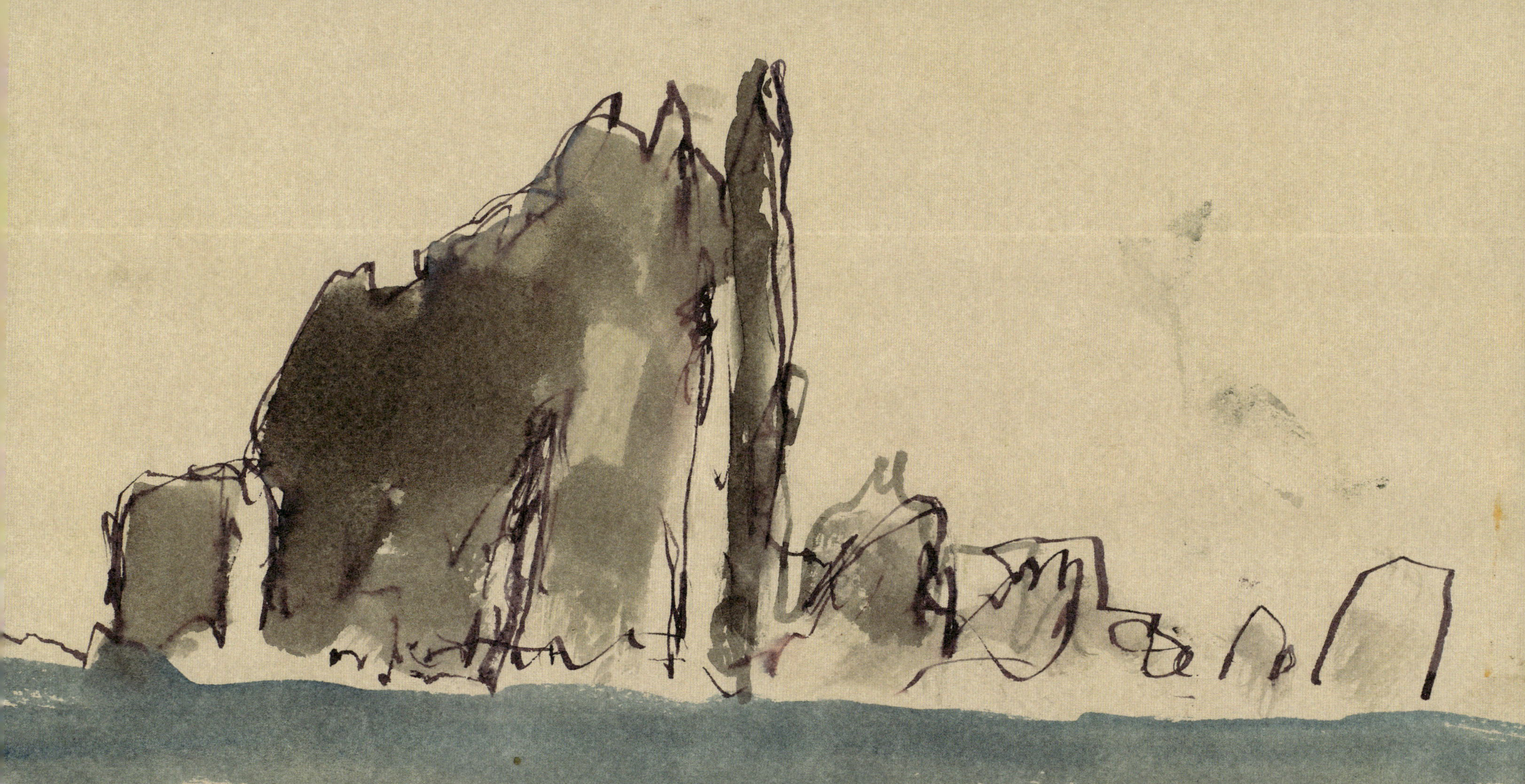

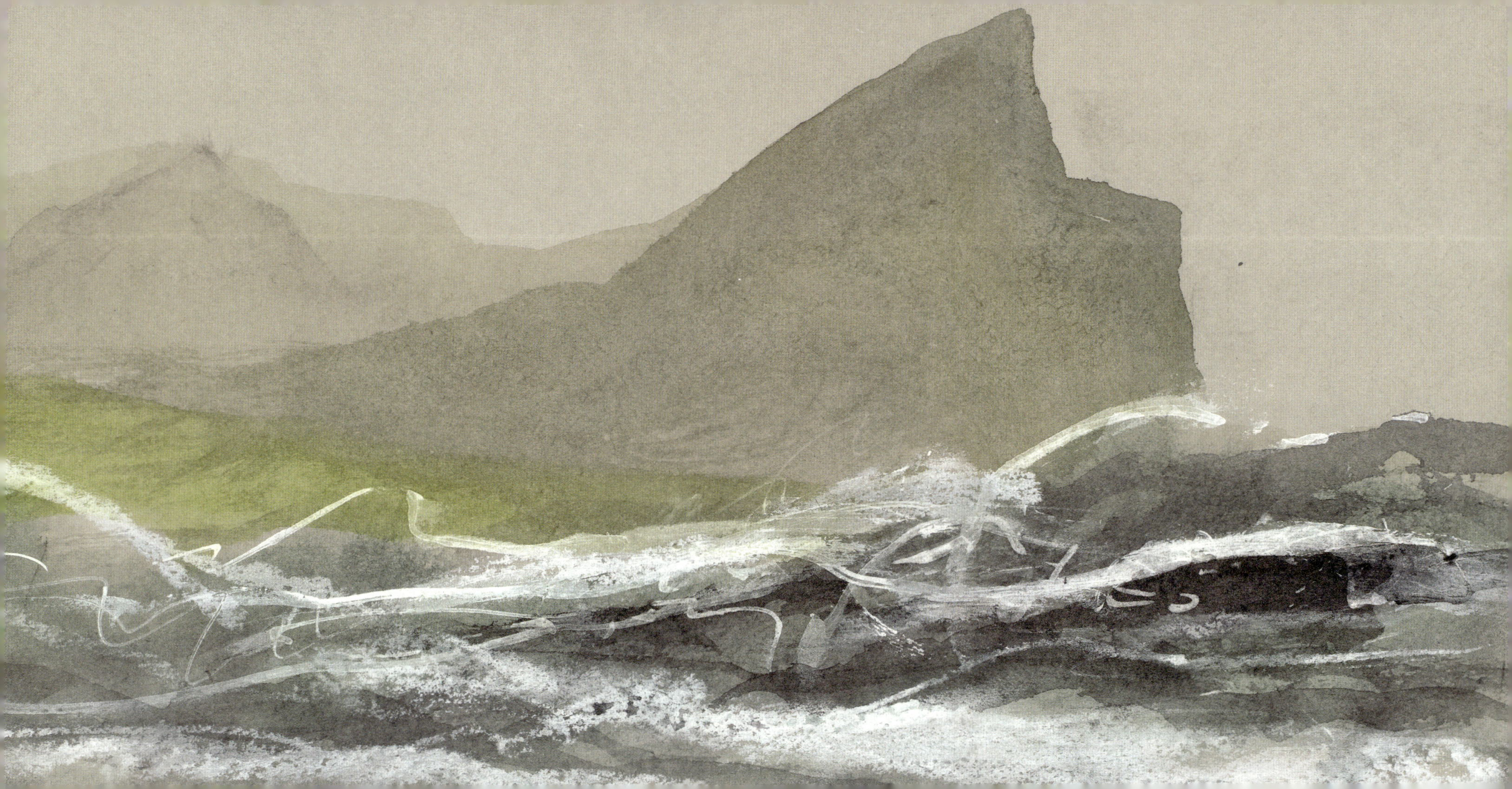

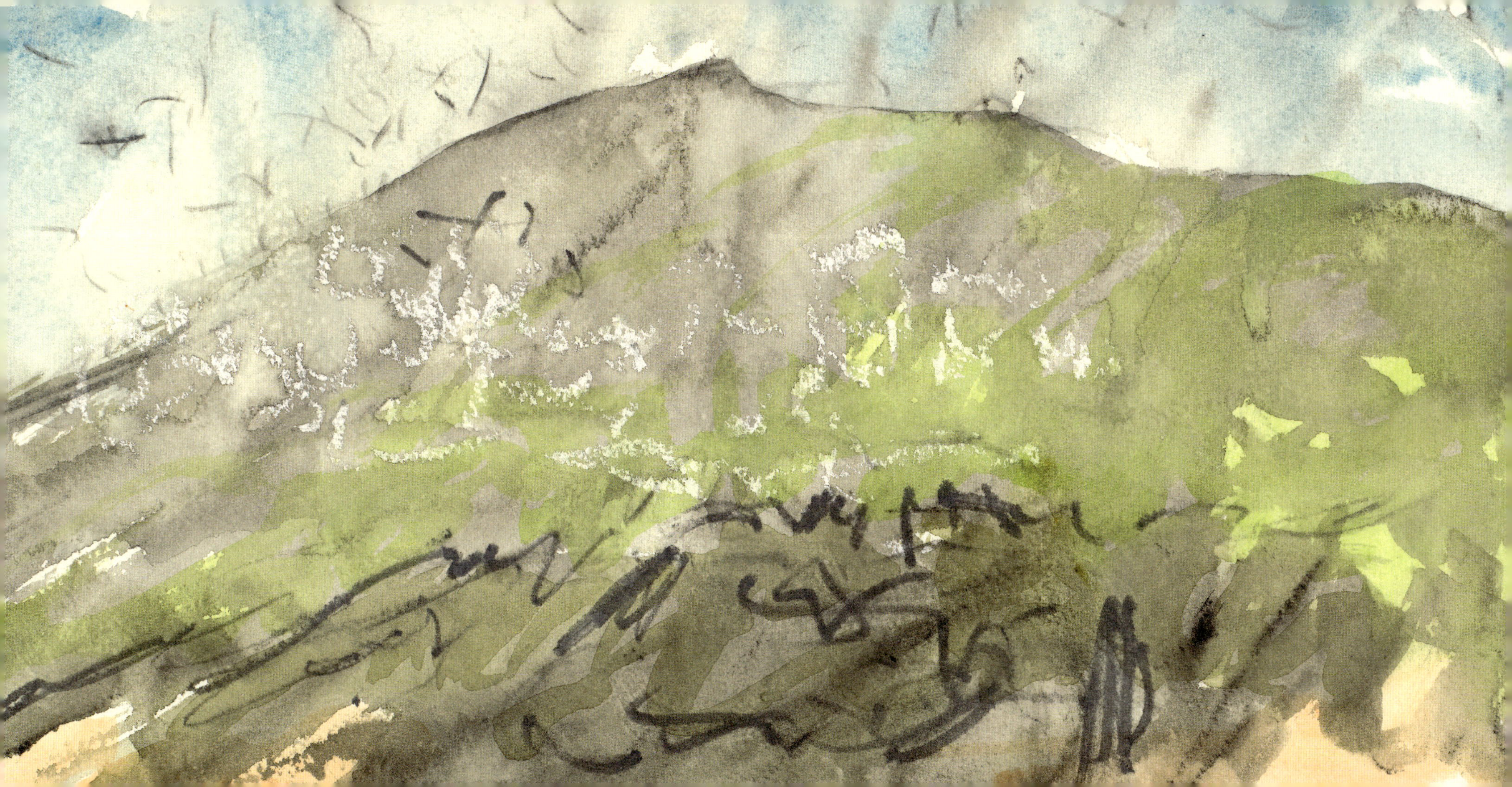

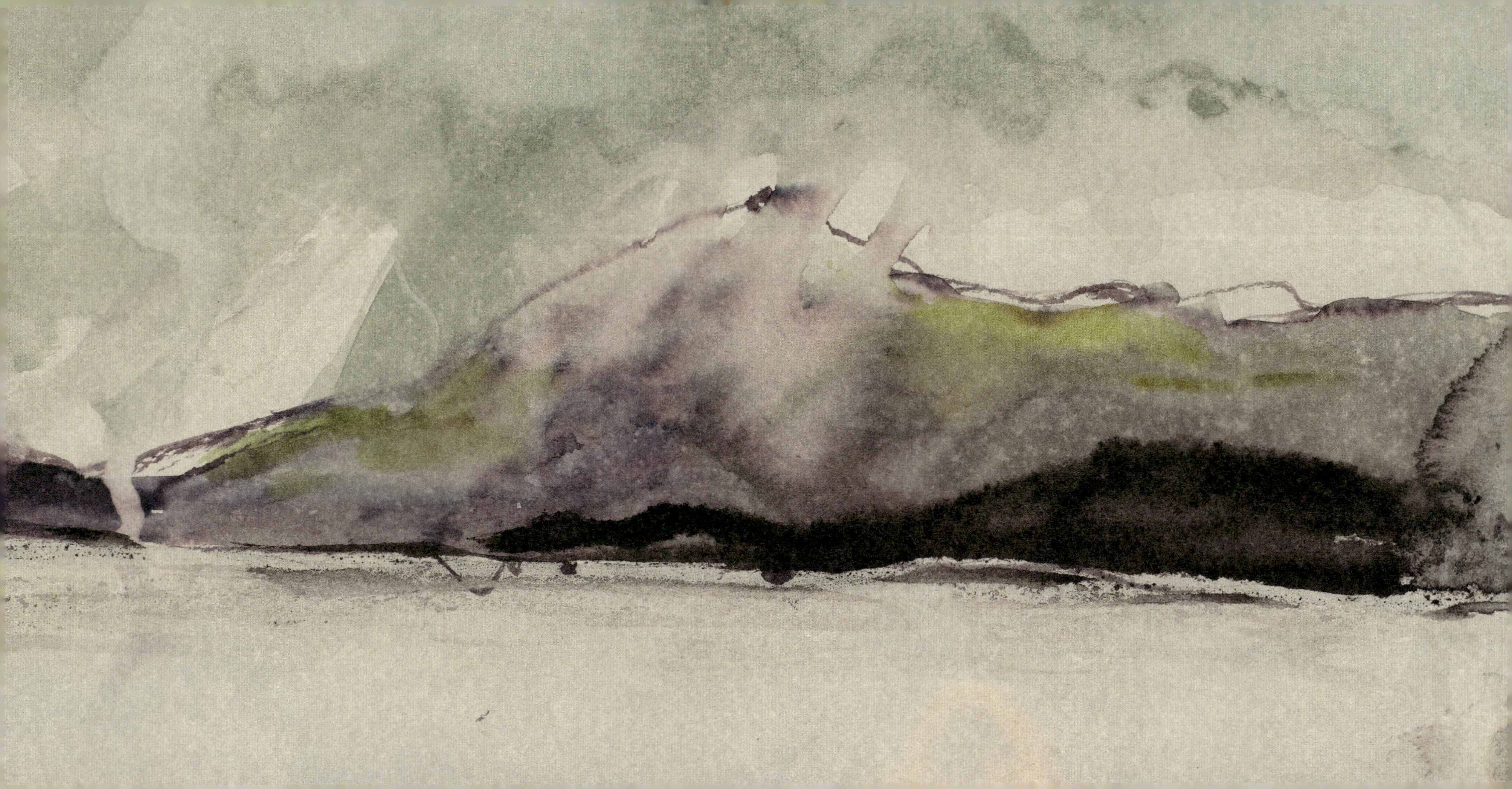

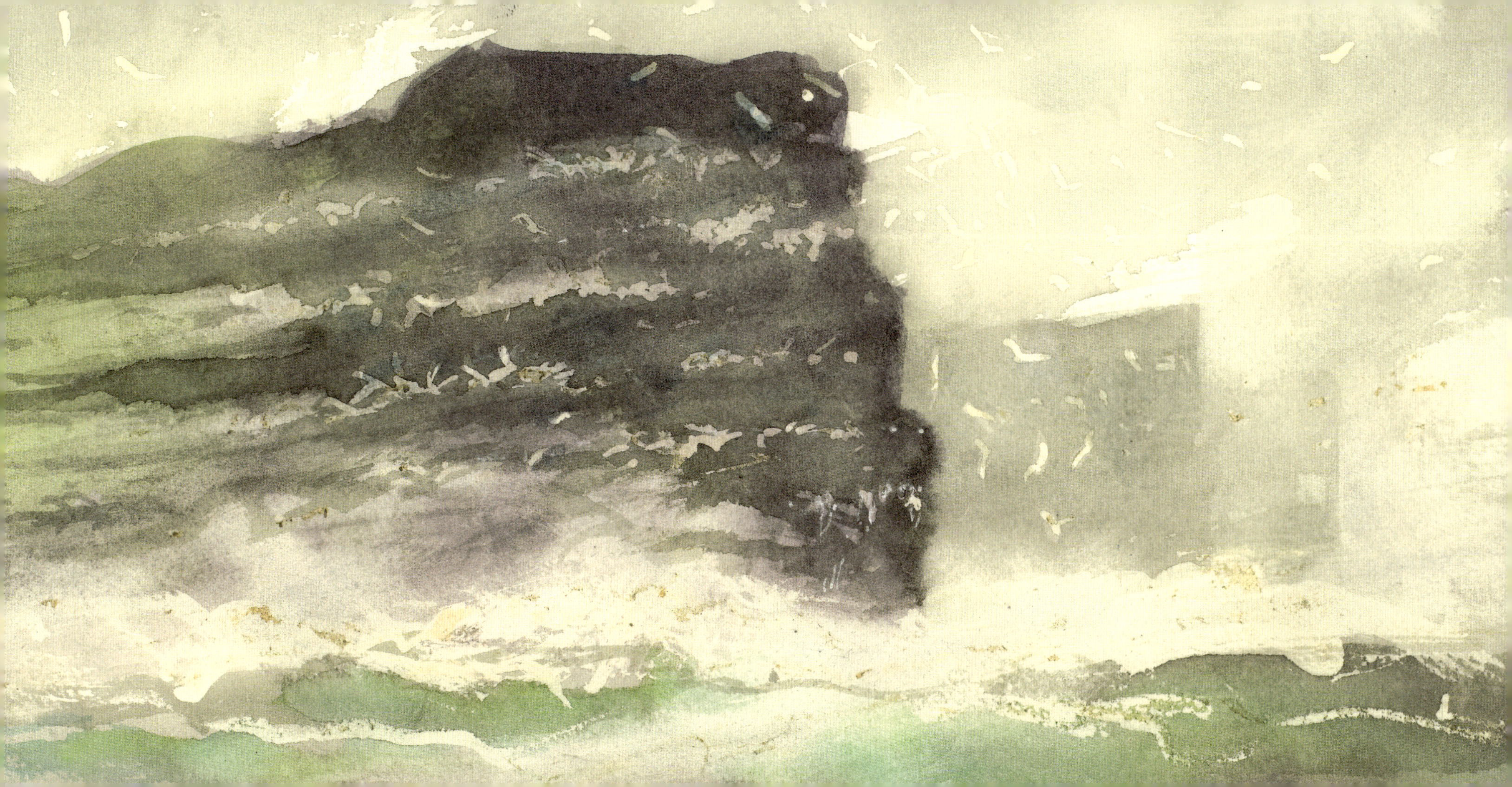

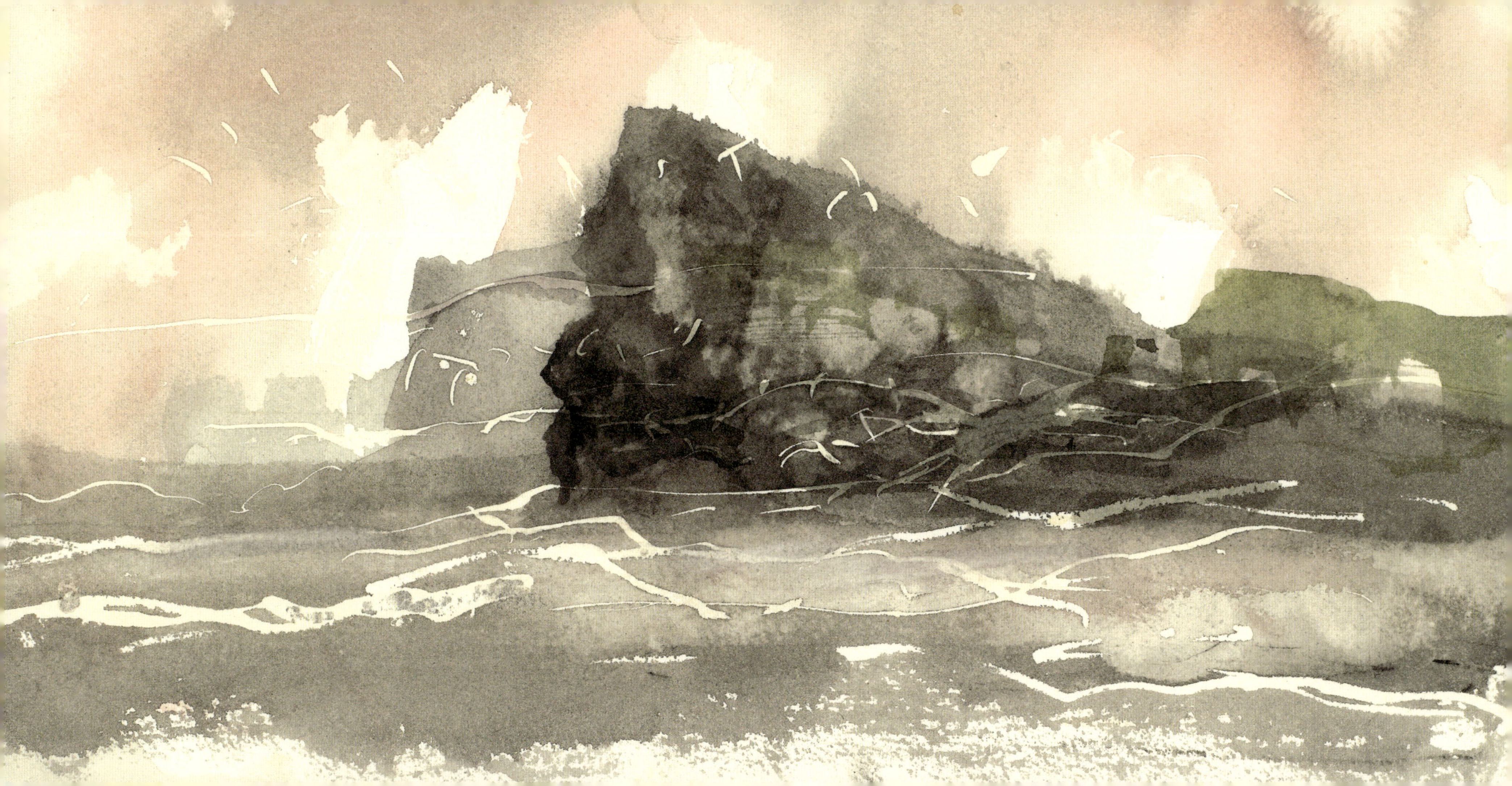

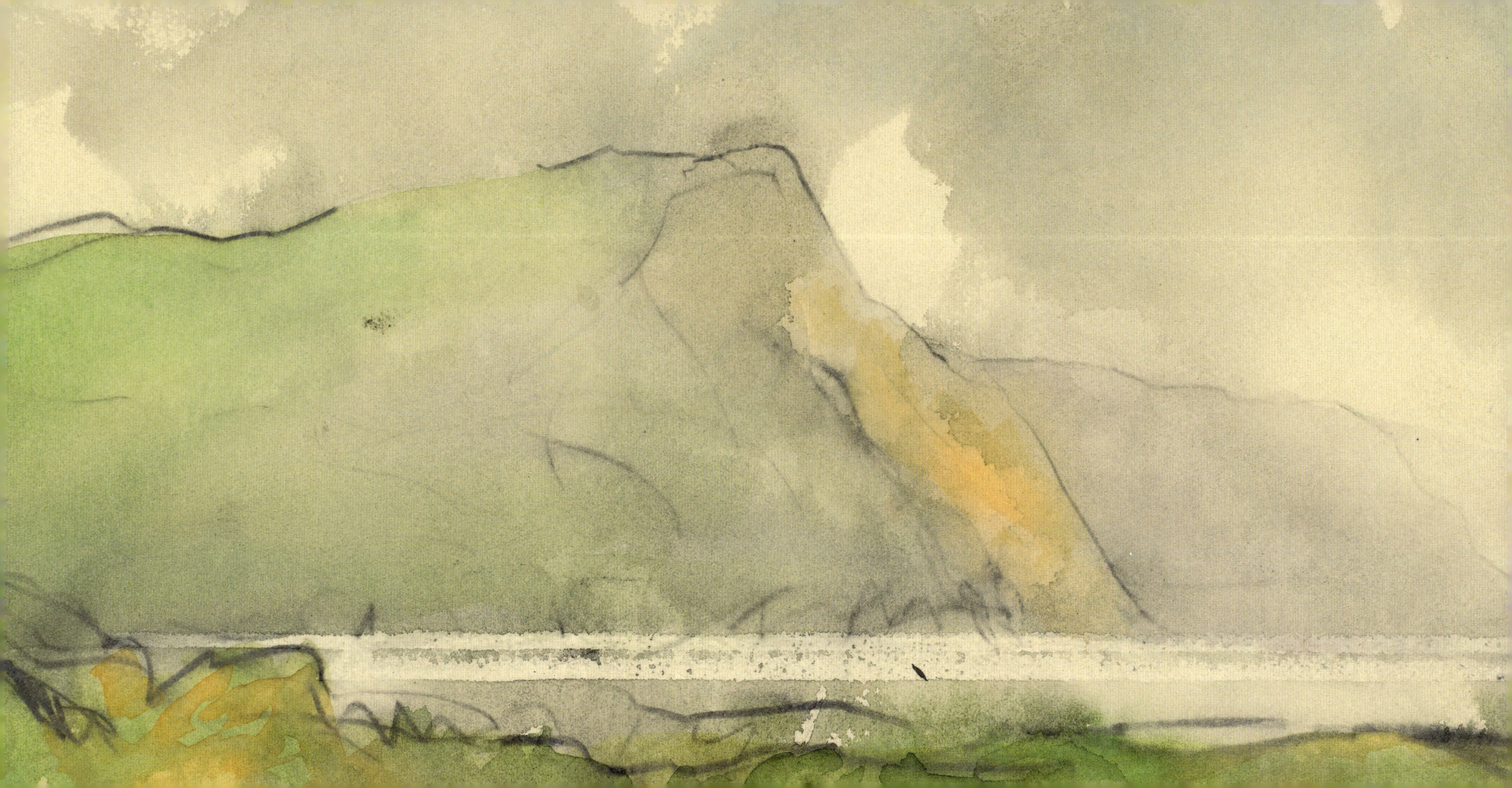

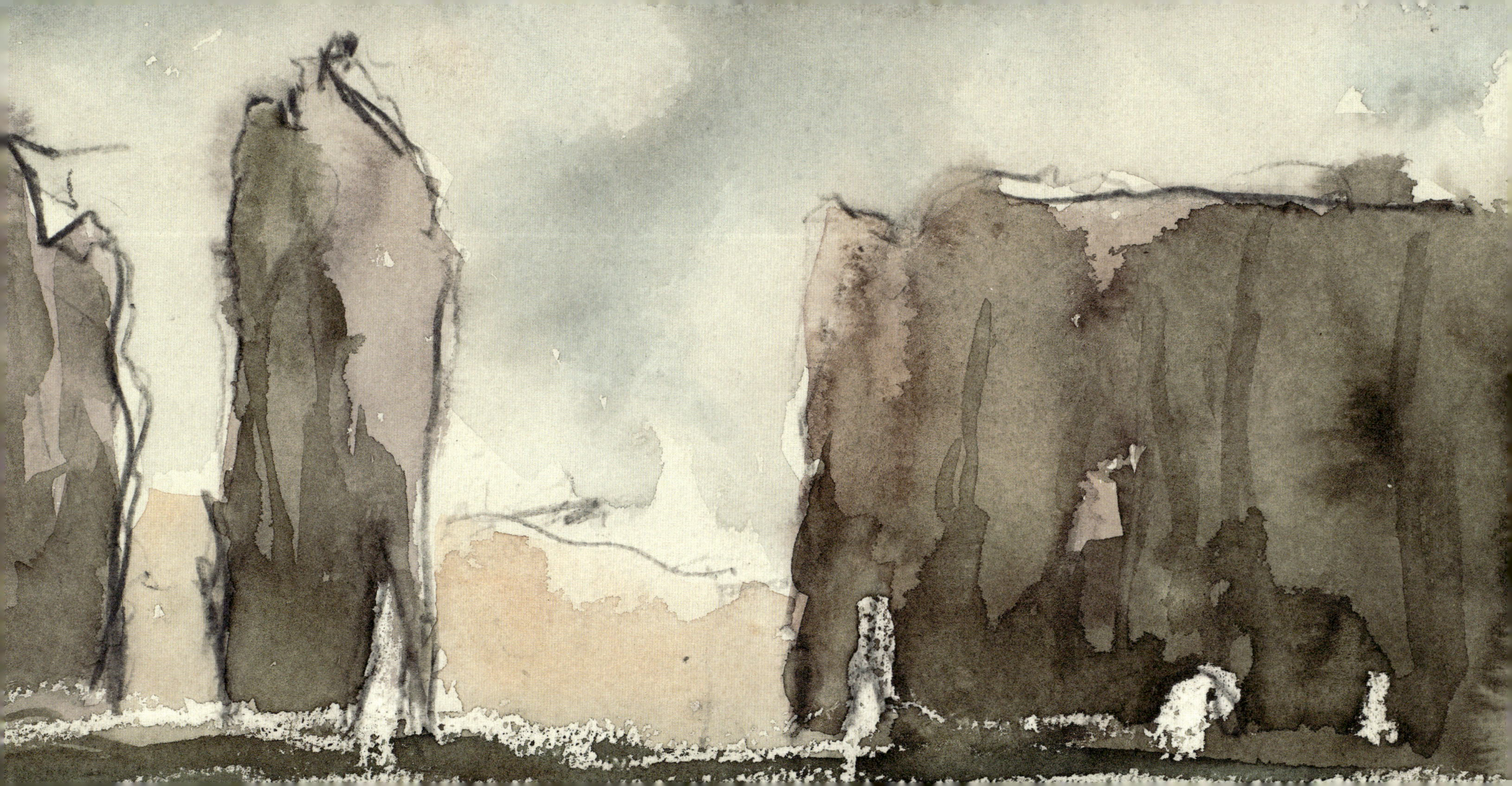

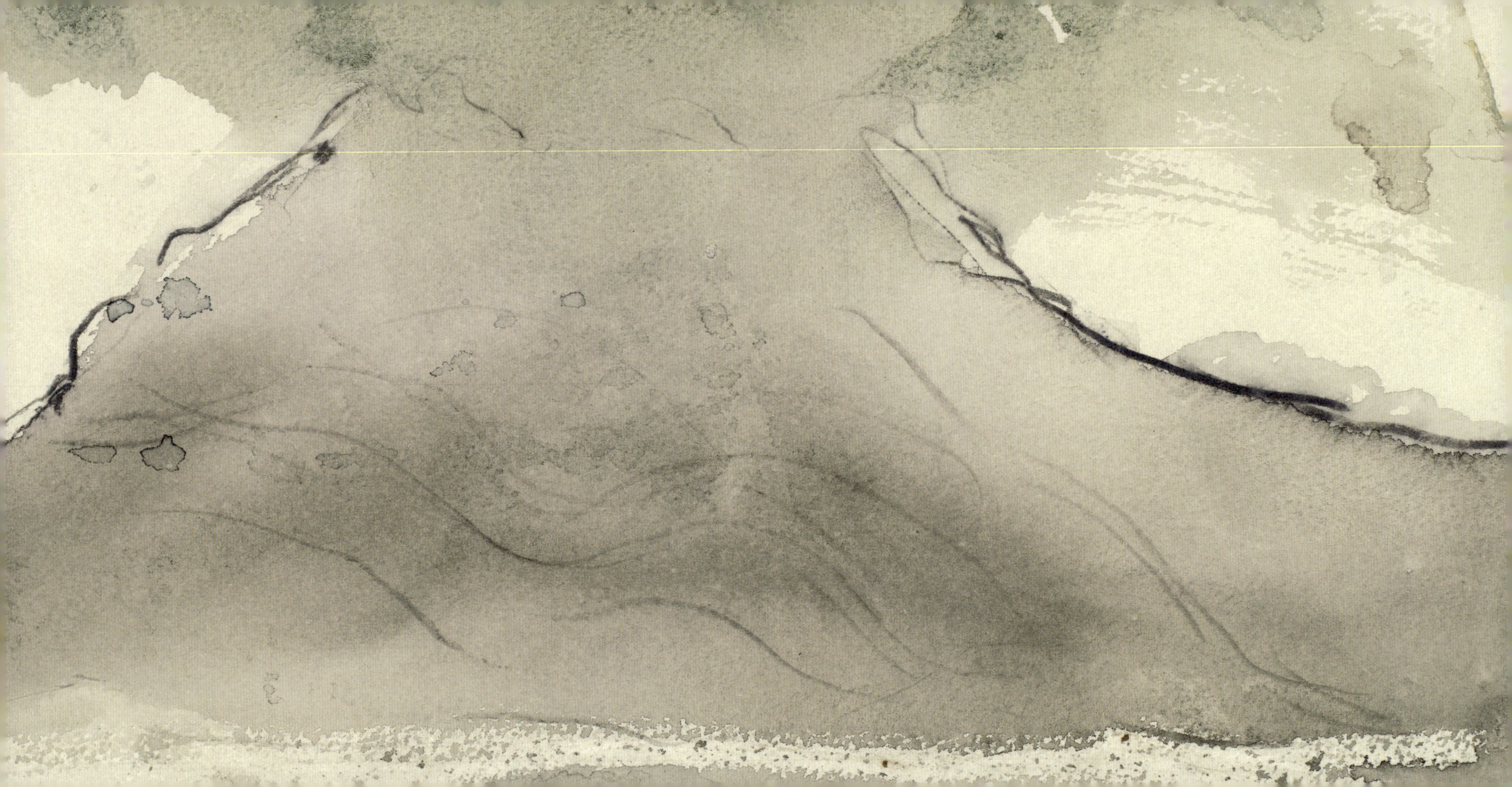

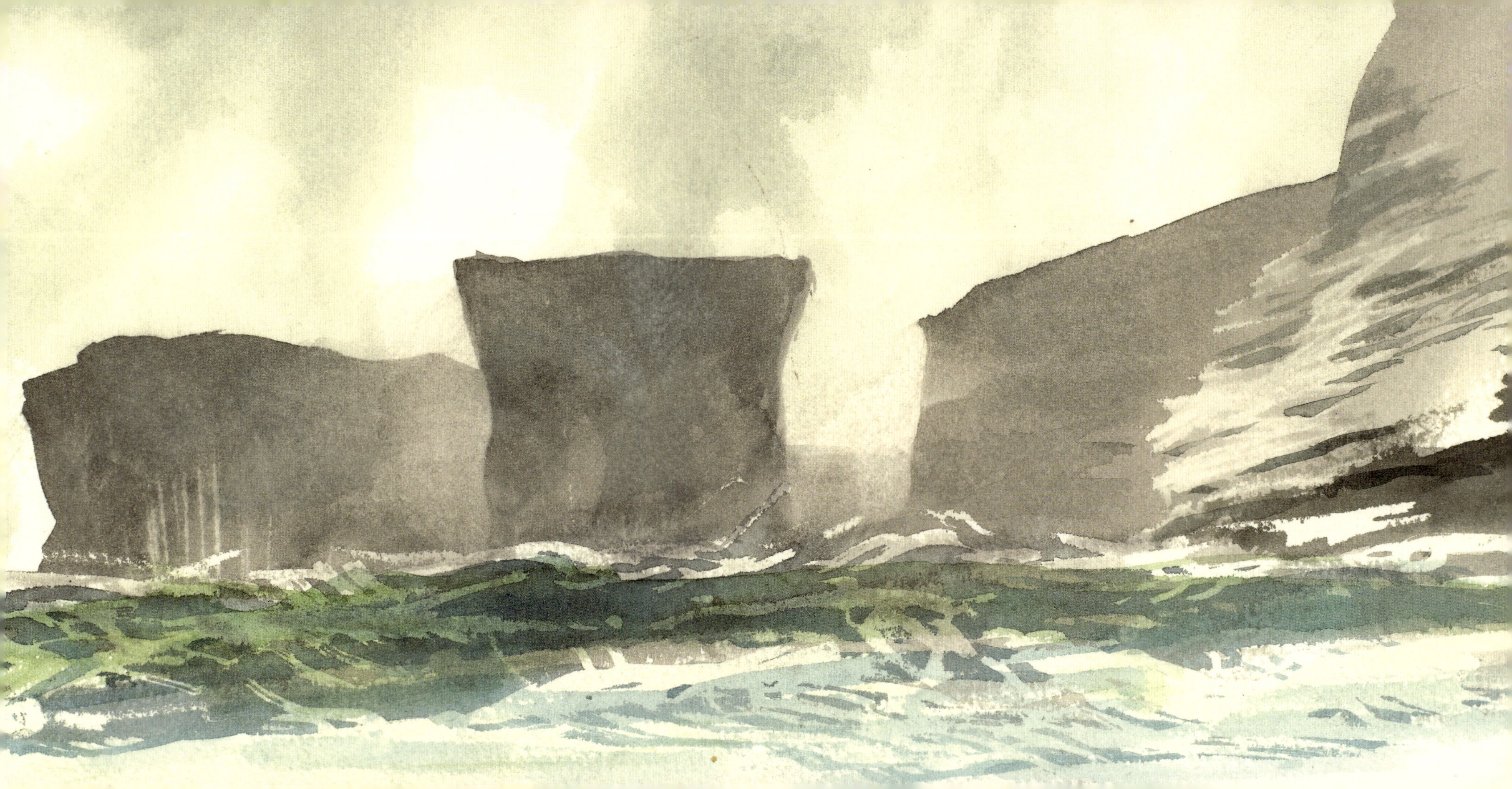

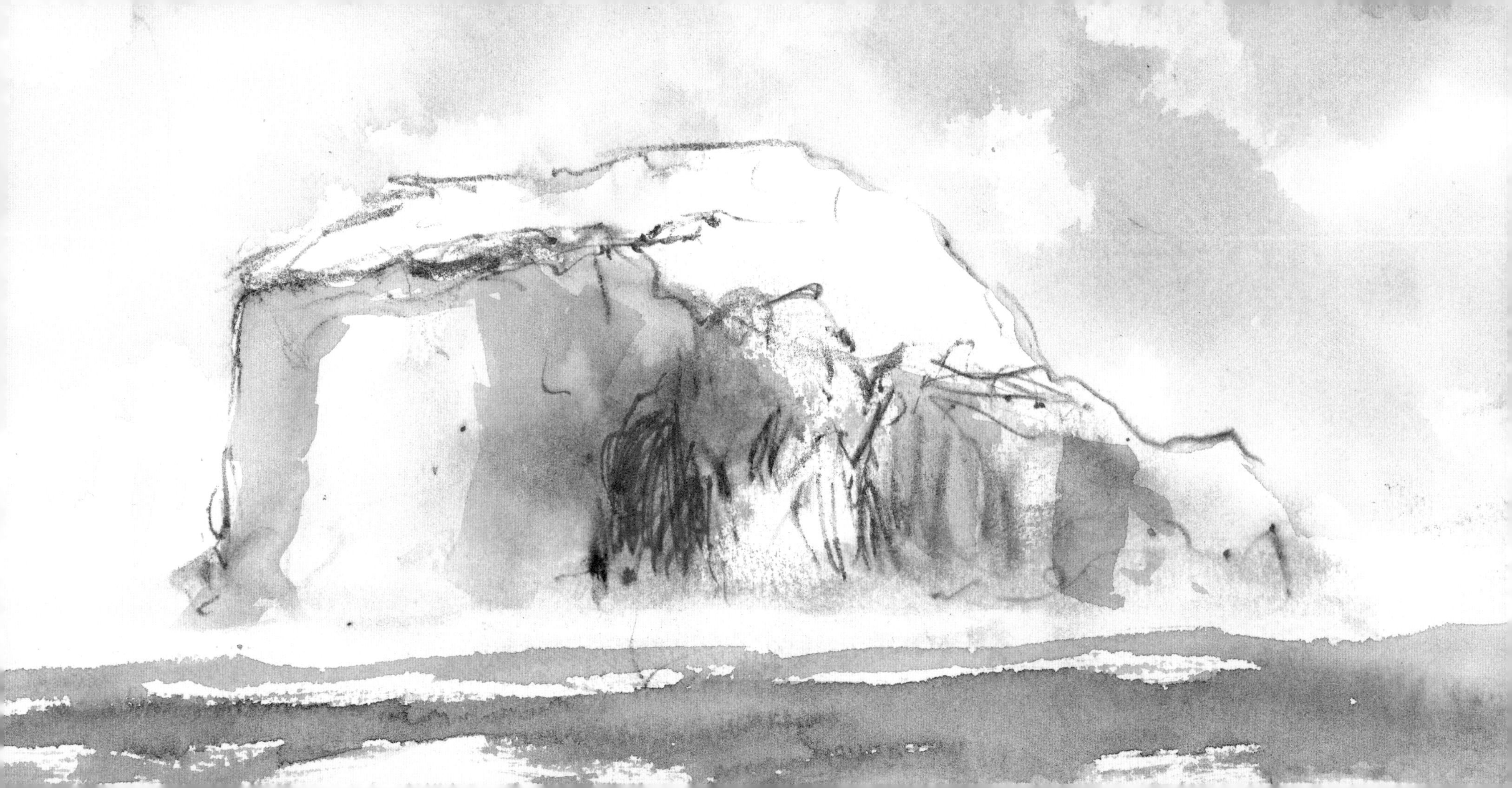

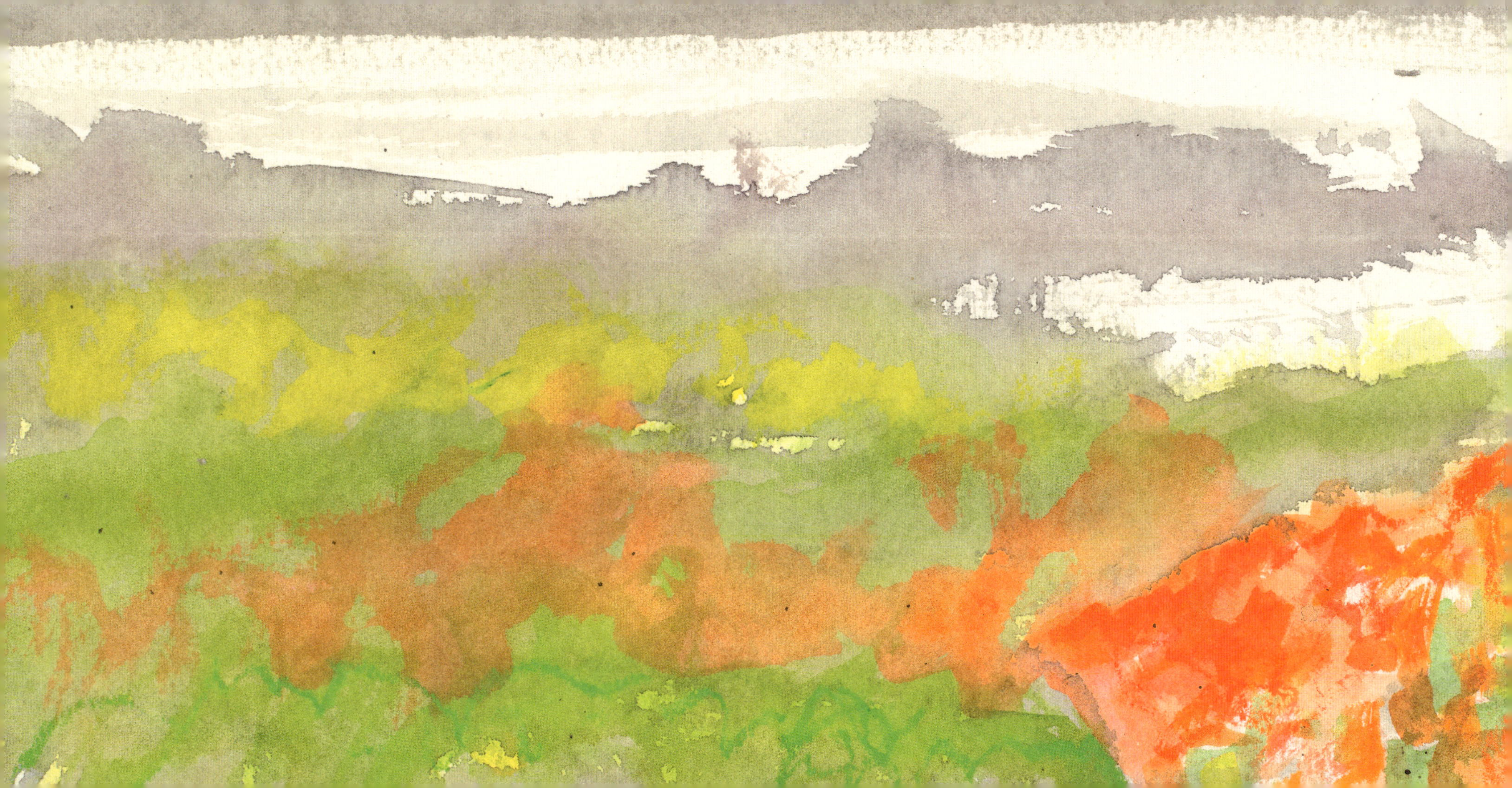

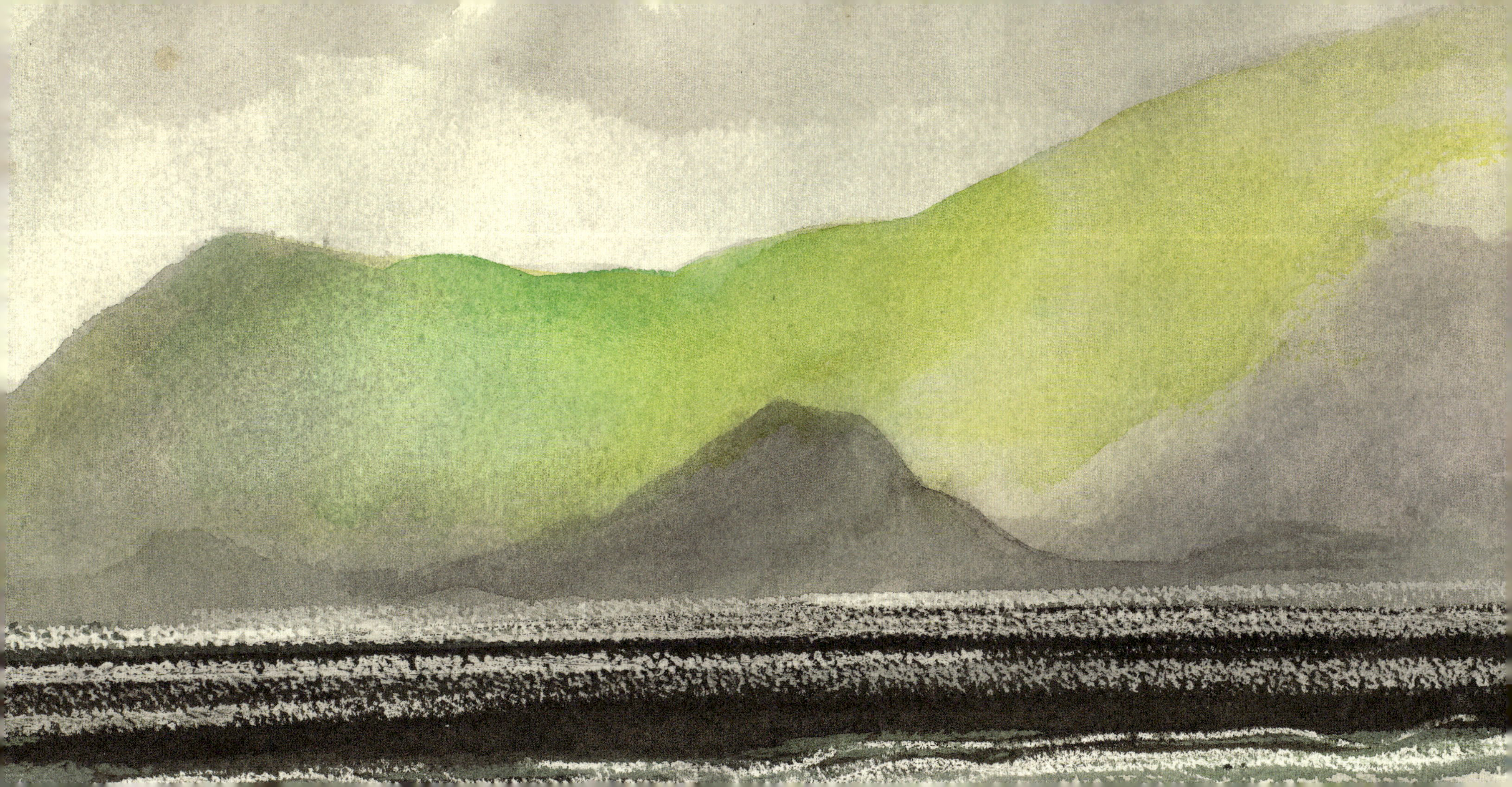

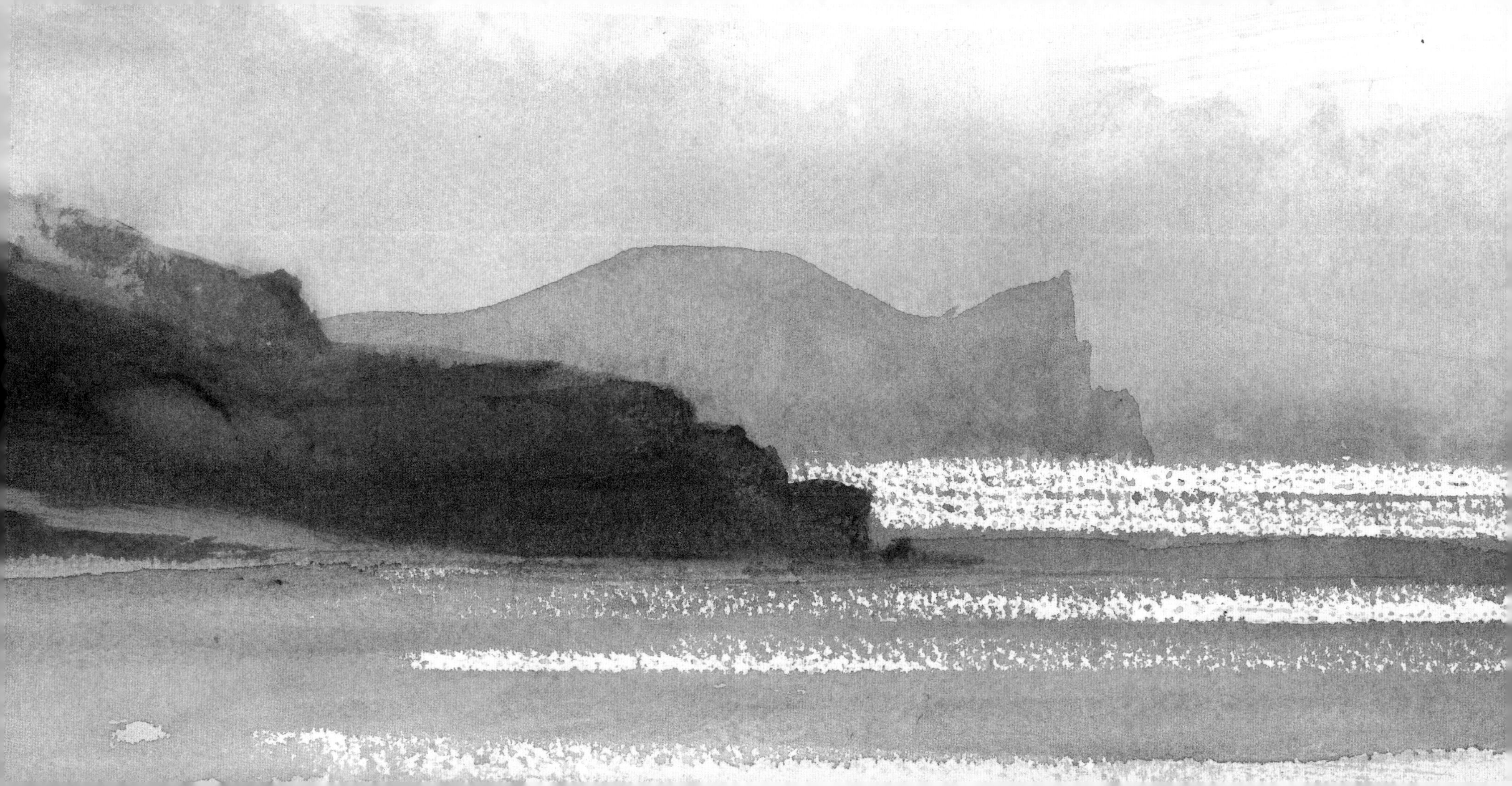

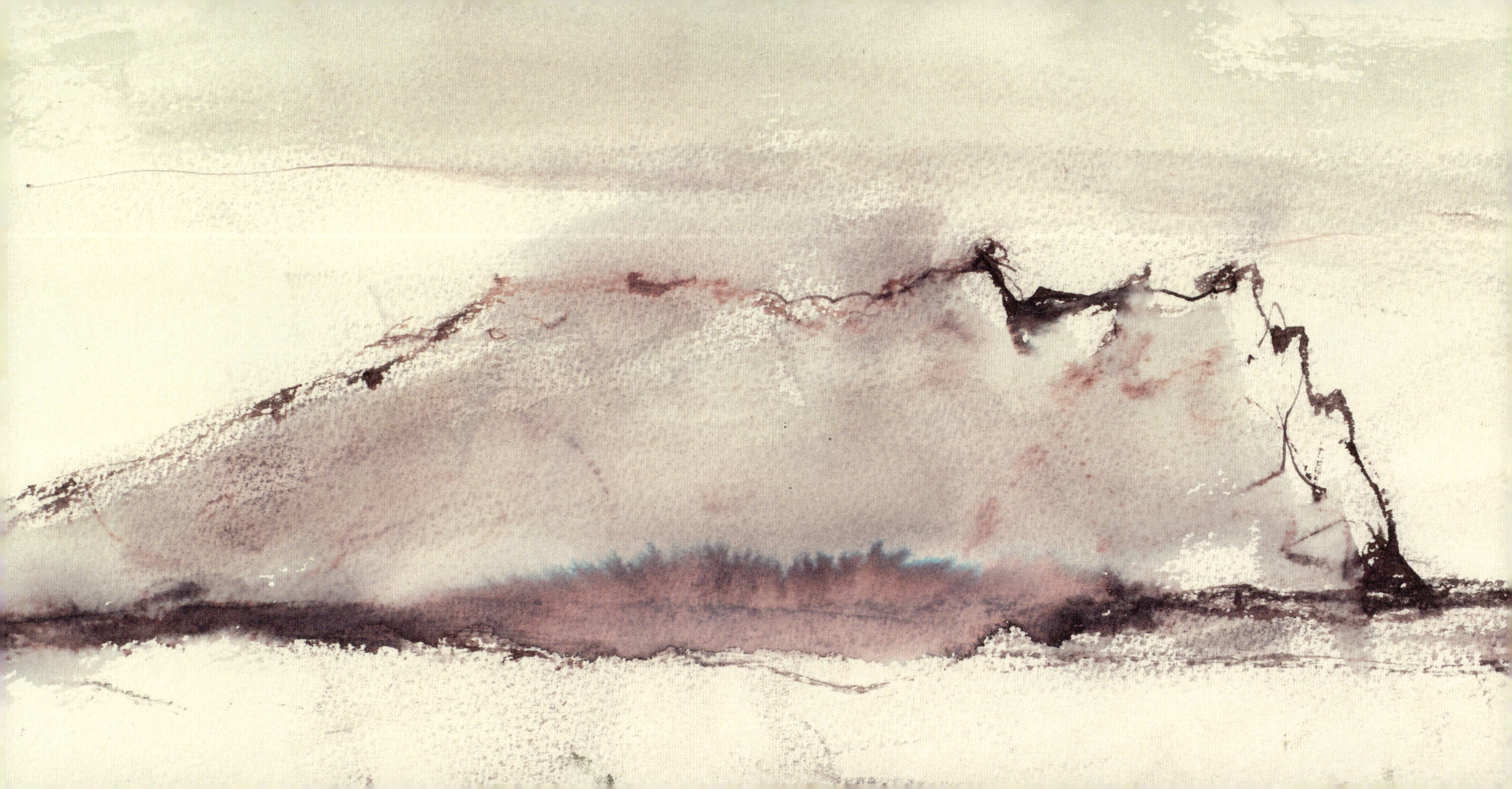

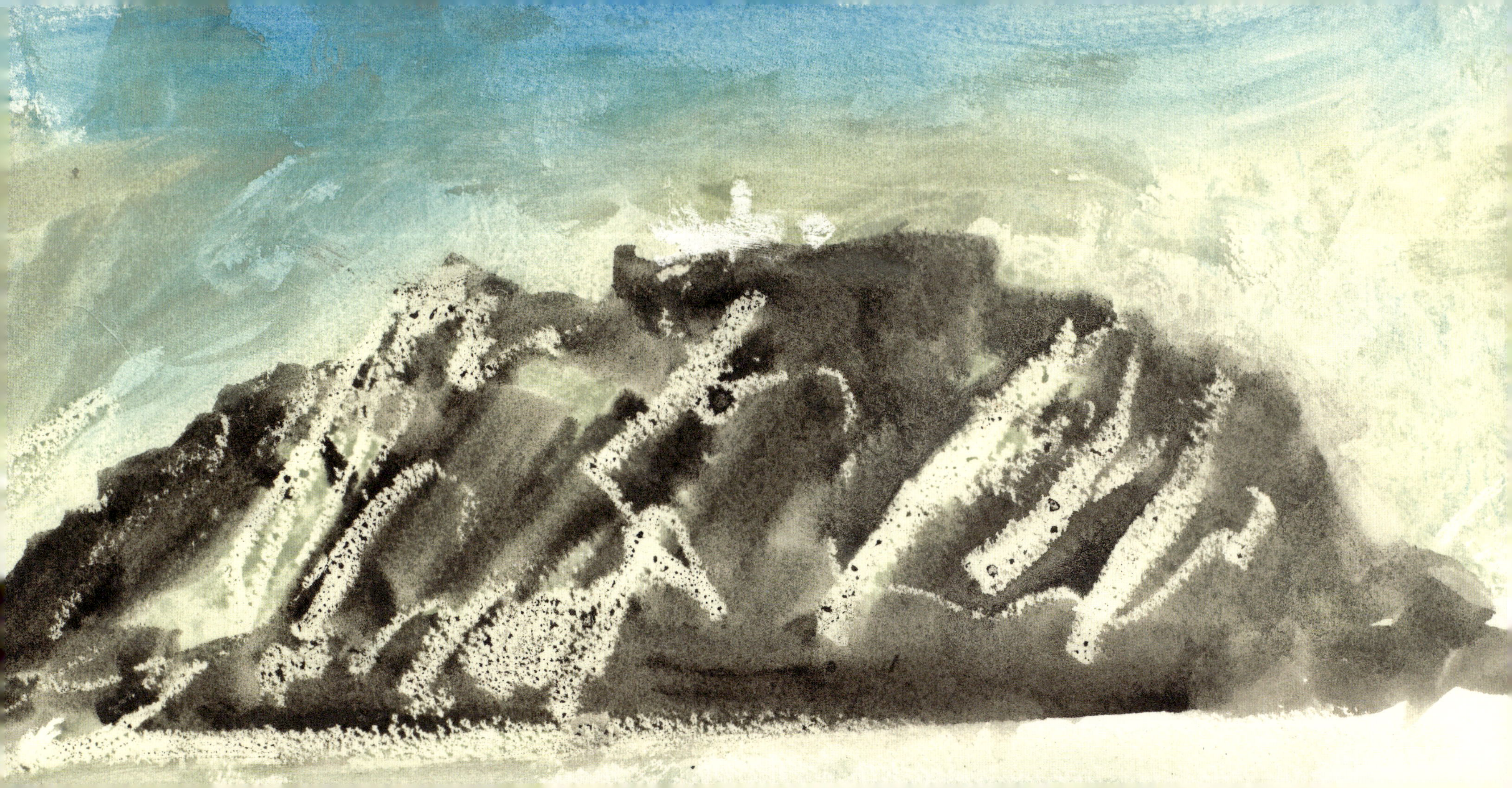

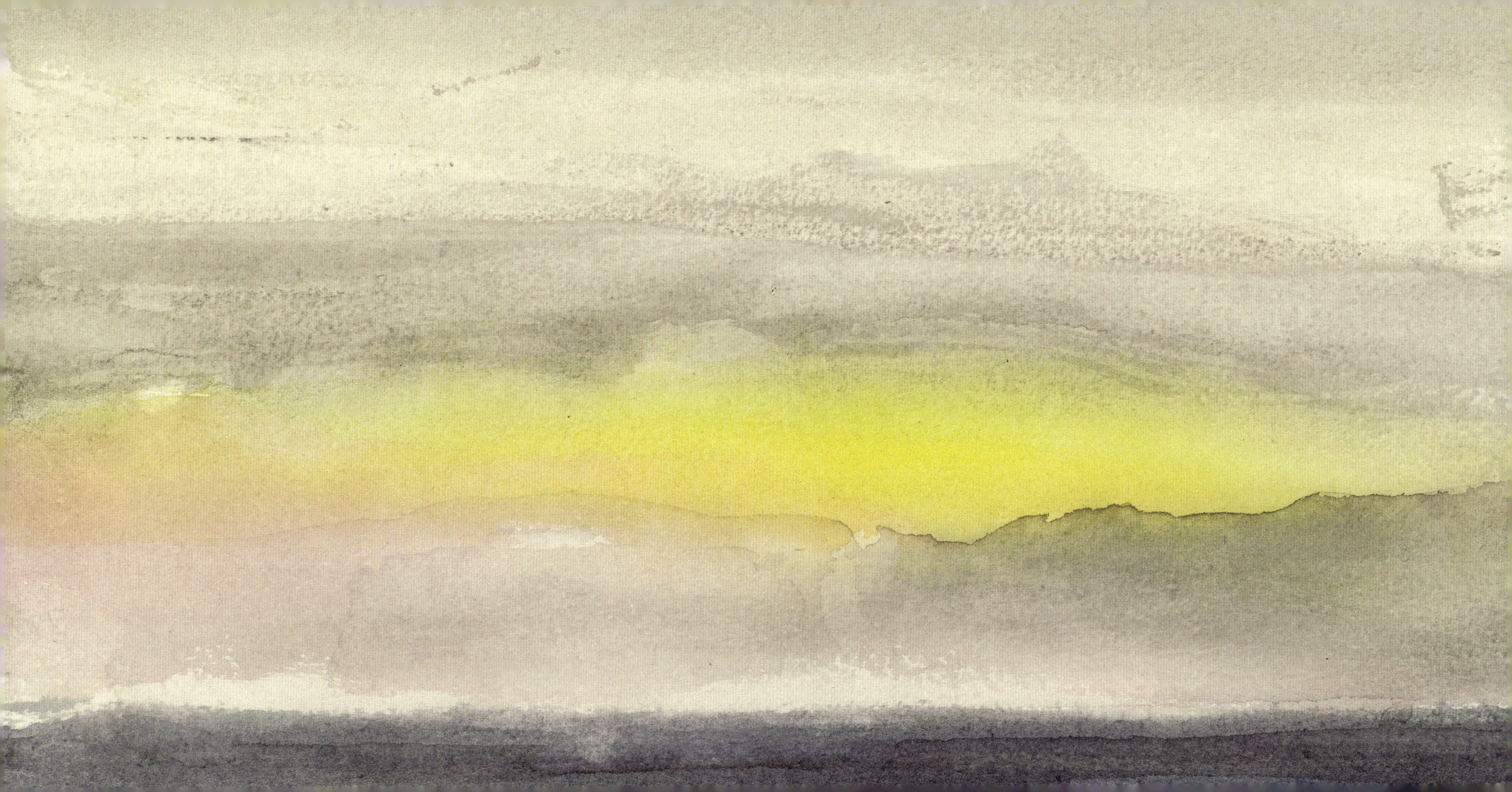

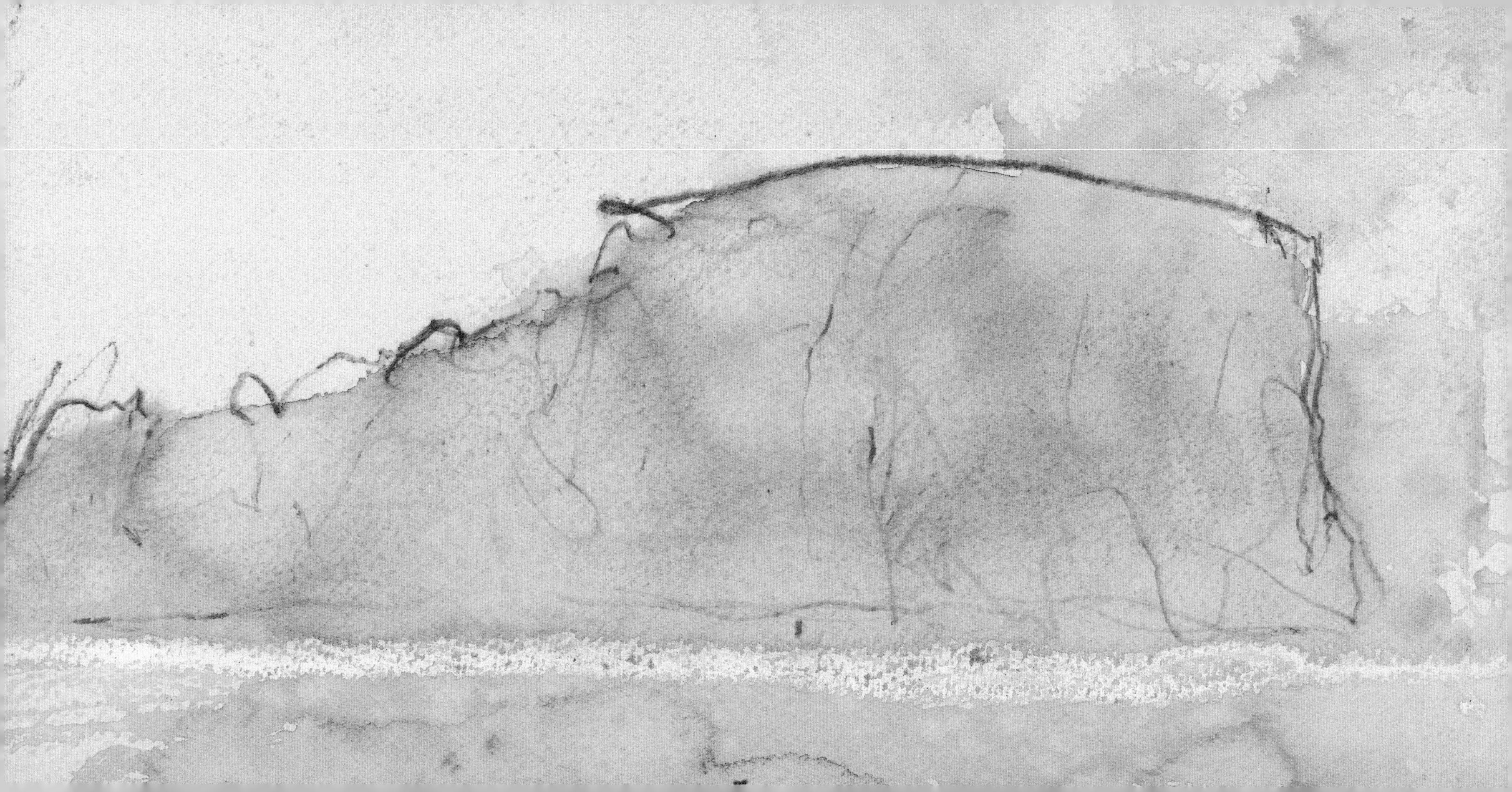

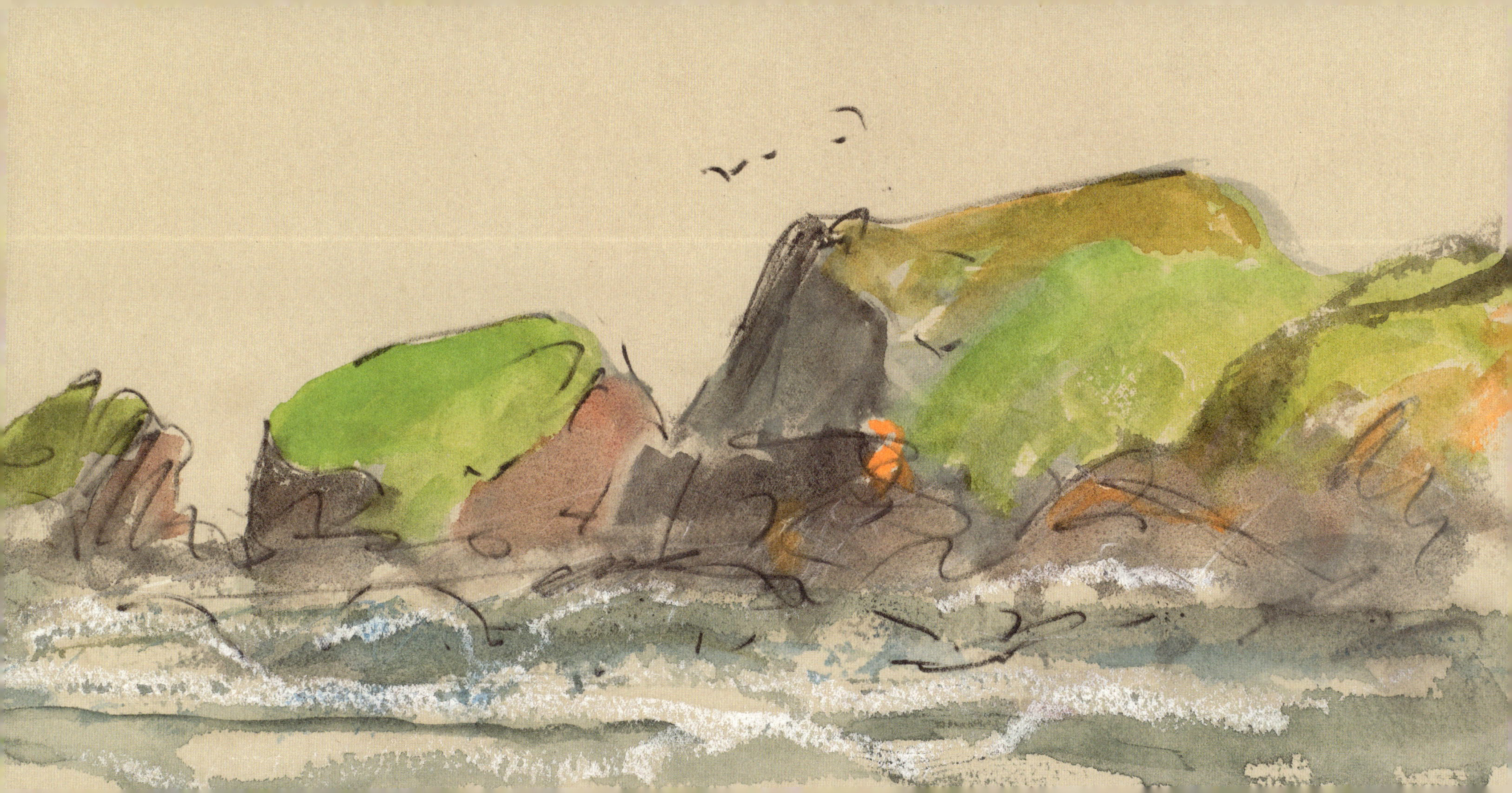

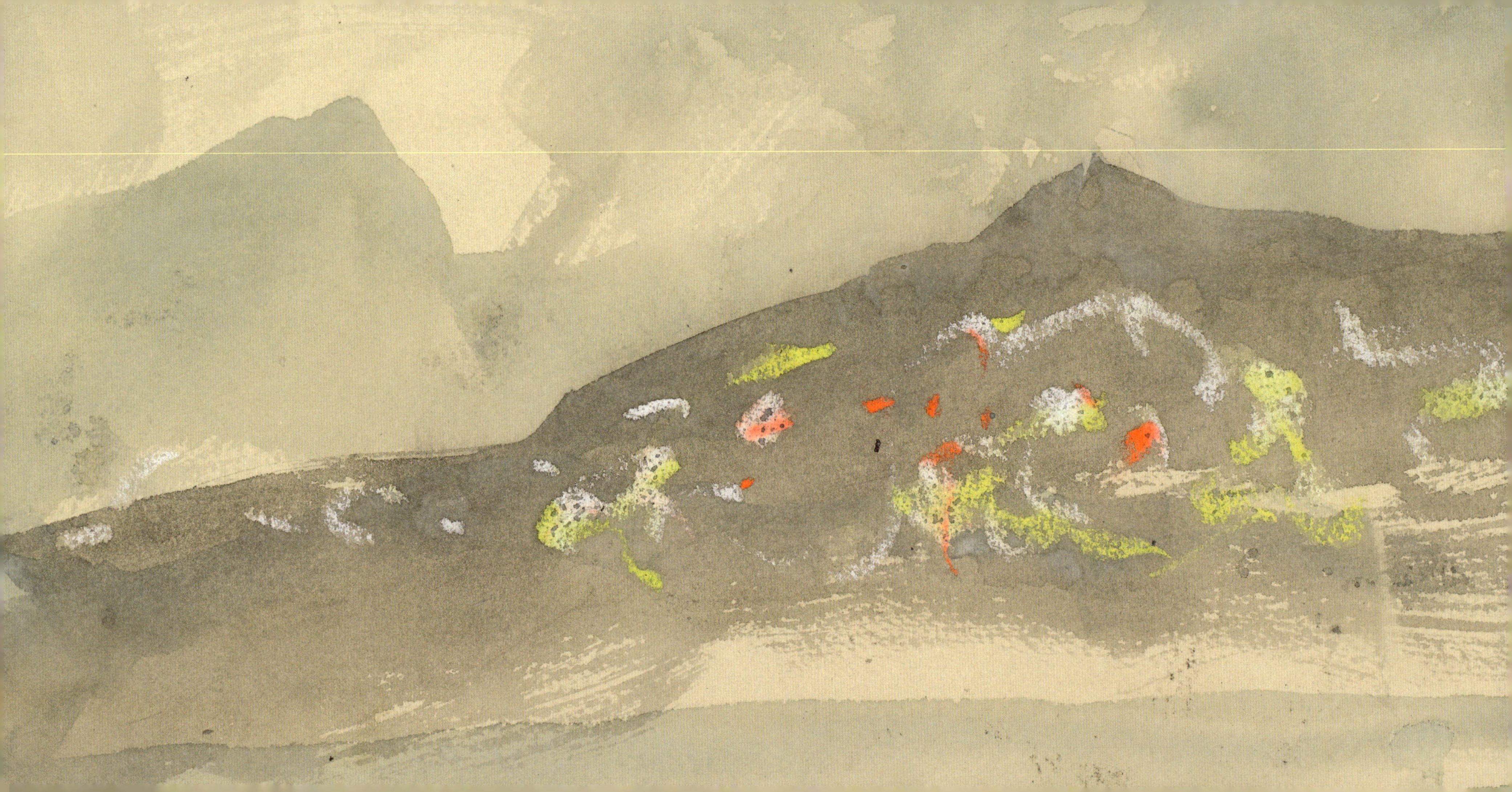

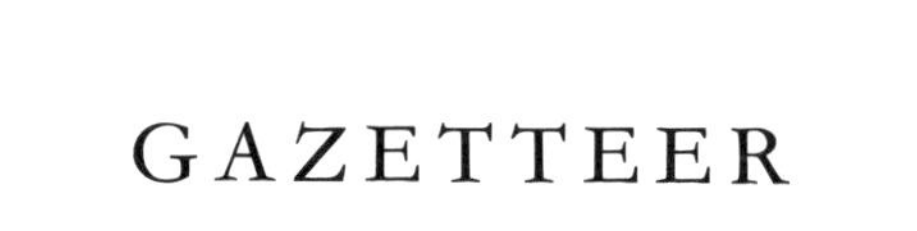

GAZETTEER

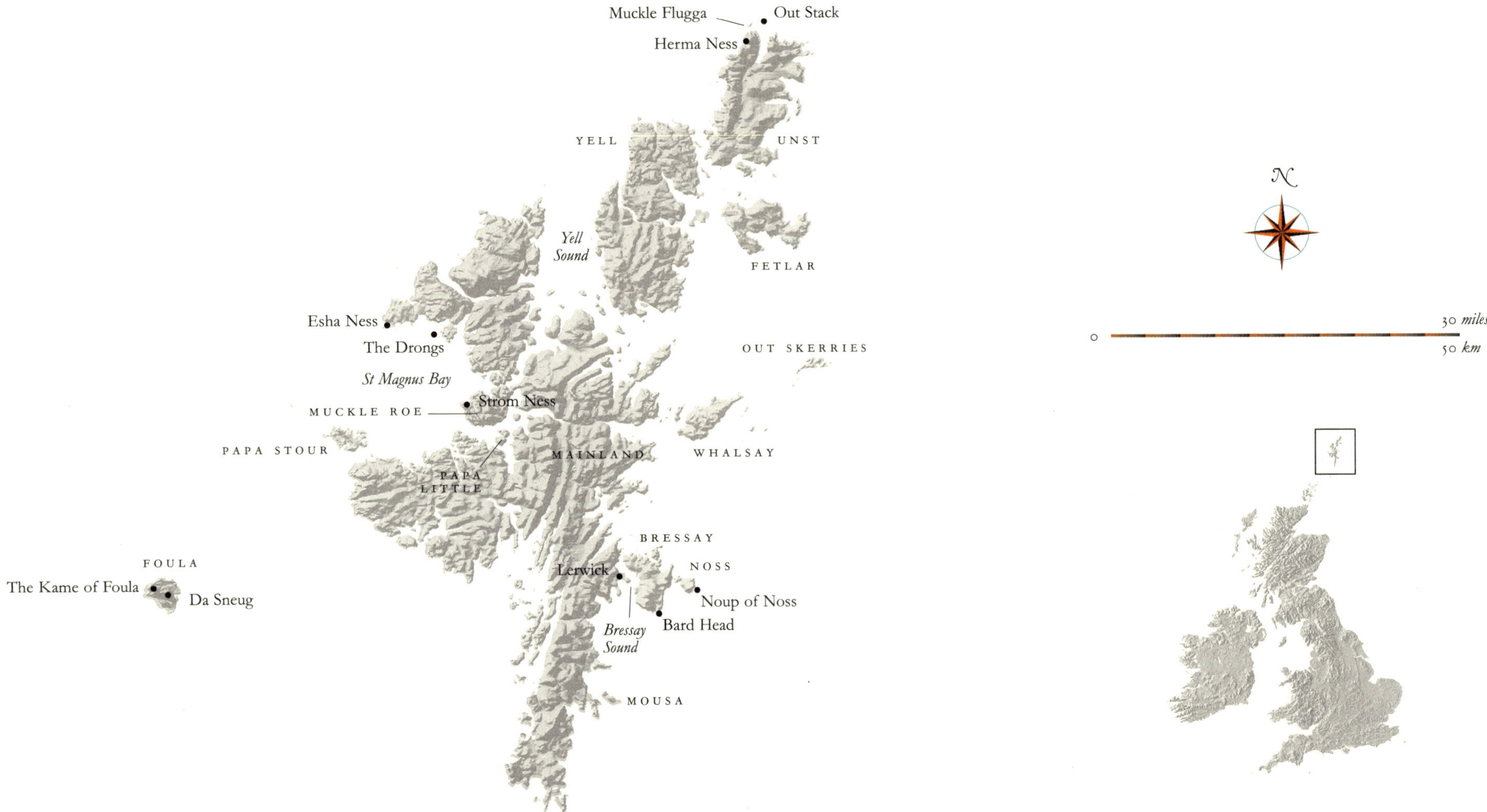
Muckle Flugga
Out Stack
Herma Ness
YELL
UNST
Yell Sound
FETLAR
Esha Ness
The Drongs
St Magnus Bay
OUT SKERRIES
Strom Ness
MUCKLE ROE
PAPA STOUR
MAINLAND
WHALSAY
PAPA LITTLE
BRESSAY
FOULA
NOSS
The Kame of Foula
Da Sneug
Lerwick
Noup of Noss
Bard Head
Bressay Sound
MOUSA
N
0
30 miles
50 km

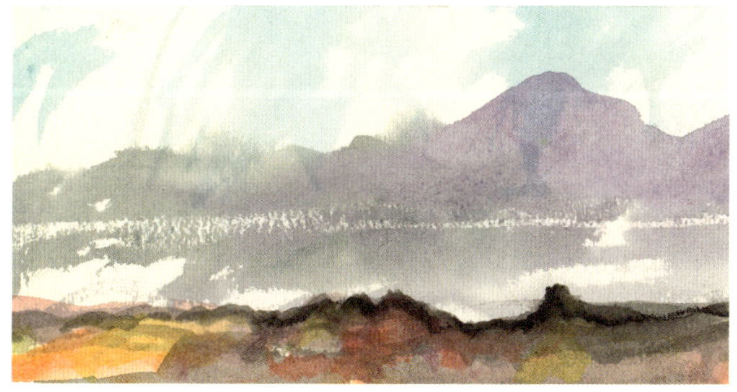

1

The cliffs of Esha Ness at the north of St Magnus Bay can be seen from the island of Muckle Roe. Ronas Hill, at 450 metres, is the highest point in Shetland.

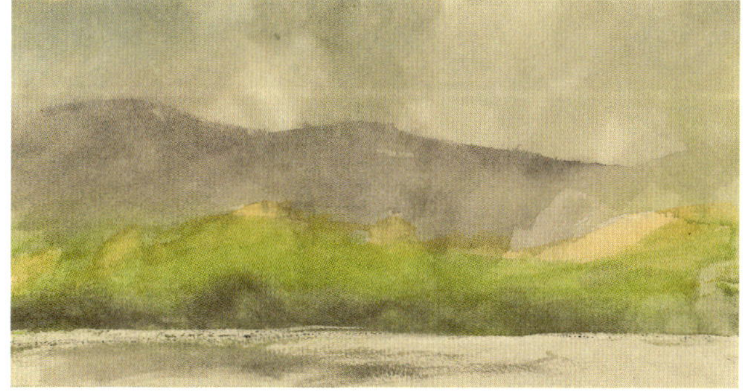

2

The west flank of the Isle of Foula is home to the three remaining families who live on the island. The families instigated and helped to build a small airstrip to link the island with Mainland Shetland.

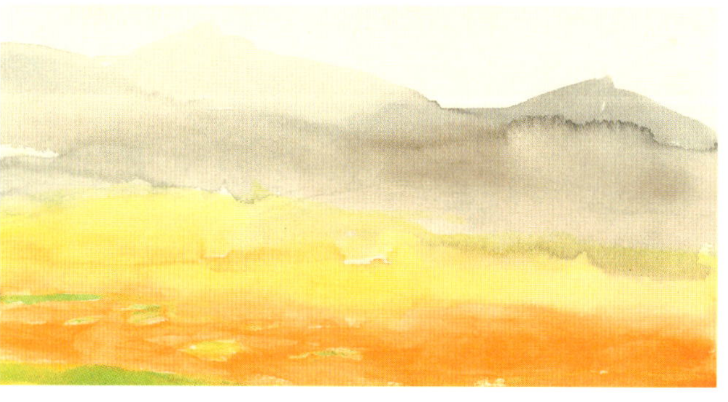

3

The island of Papa Stour has sheep and crops and extensive archaeological remains. The ritualistic Papa Stour Sword Dance dates from medieval times and is still performed regularly throughout the United Kingdom.

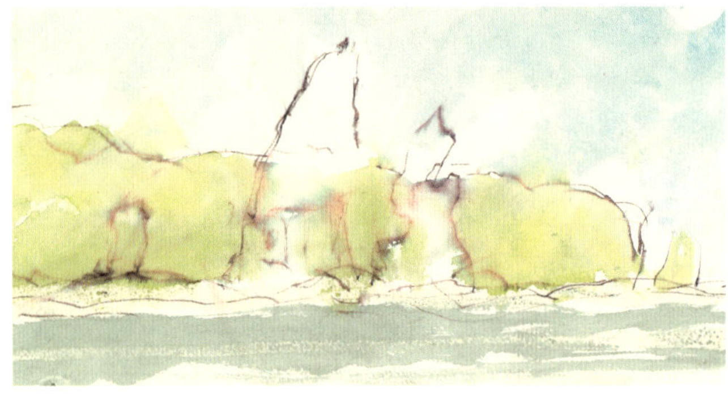

4

The Drongs are one of several grotesque rock formations standing off the cliffs of Esha Ness.

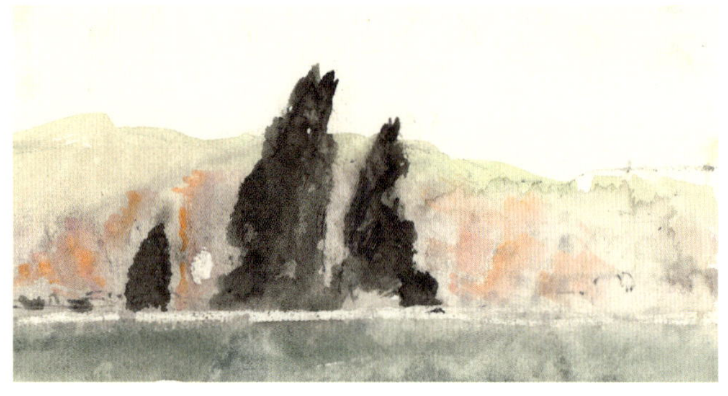

5

The Drongs take on many forms in different lights, with the soft pink cliffs of Esha Ness to the north.

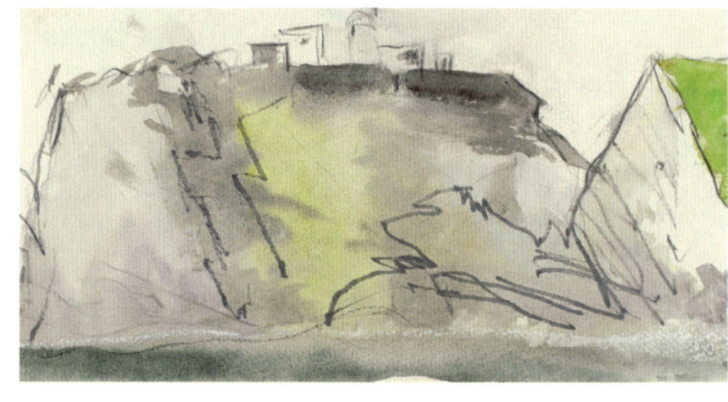

6

The steps up to the lighthouse on Muckle Flugga can only be accessed in suitable conditions. This is the northernmost Stevenson lighthouse in the British Isles.

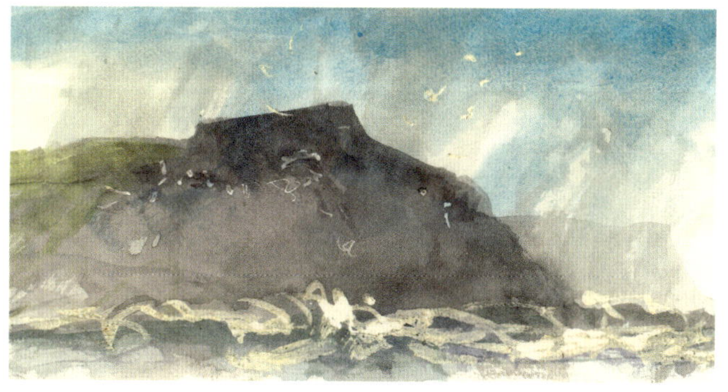

7

The Kame of Foula appears in the distance when circumnavigating the south-east of the island.

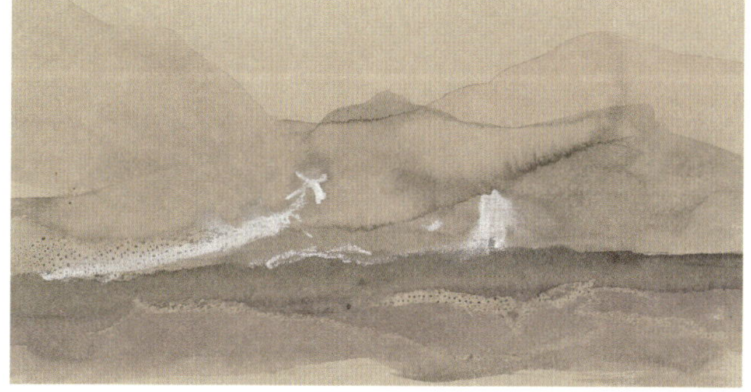

8

From the south-west, Foula appears ethereal and almost transparent. Da Sneug, at 418 metres, is the second highest peak in Shetland.

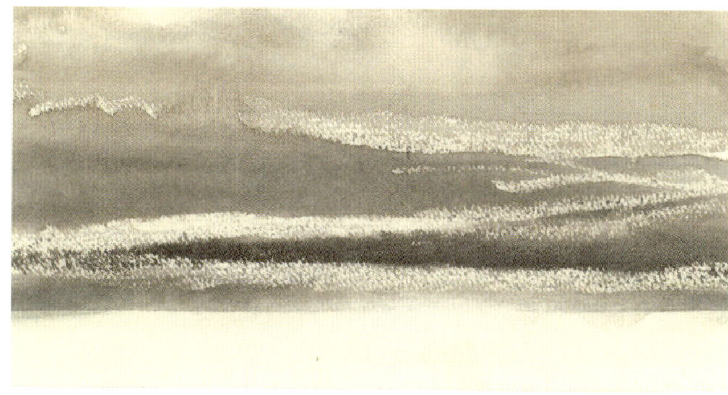

9

Even on a calm day the open, unfettered ocean off the cliffs of Esha Ness holds a permanent deep Atlantic swell.

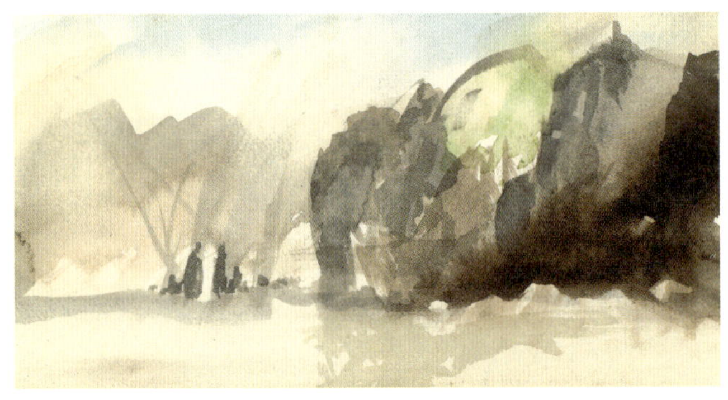

10

The soft cliffs of Esha Ness, topped by a spectacular Stevenson lighthouse, are being constantly carved and undercut by the Atlantic.

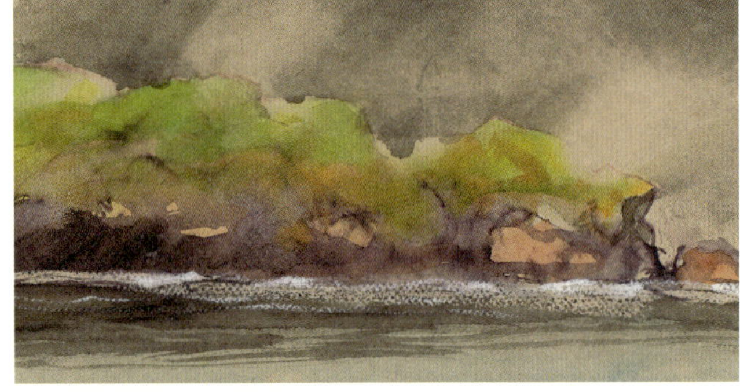

11

The island of Muckle Roe, about three miles in diameter, contains several secluded farmsteads and sheep runs and is surprisingly fertile.

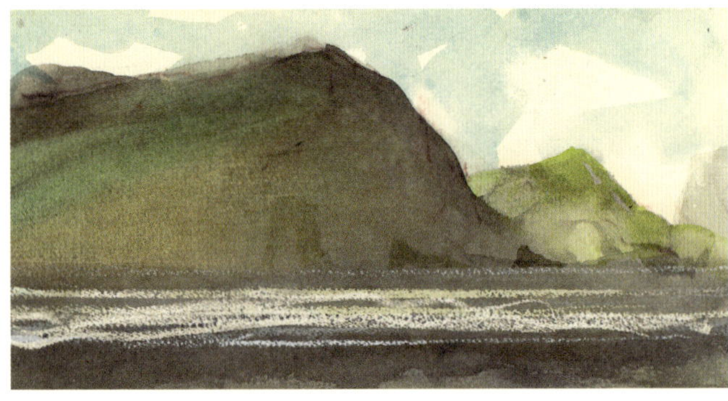

12

The Hill of Setter on Noss can be seen behind Bard Head on Bressay. A stud farm was established on Noss in the nineteenth century to supply Shetland ponies for the Northumberland coalfields.

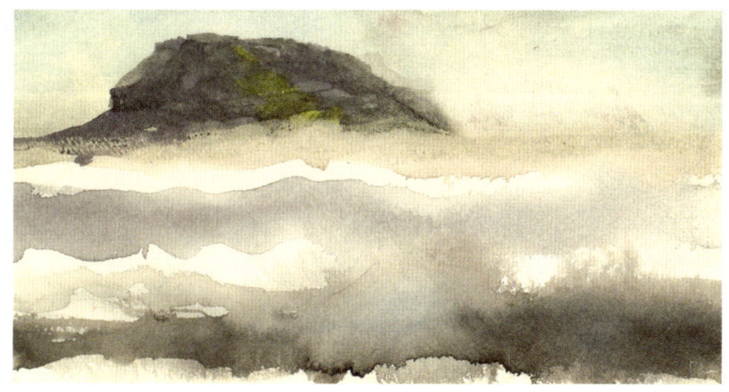

13

Lying a few hundred yards north-east of Muckle Flugga, Out Stack is the most northerly land of the United Kingdom. The rock was occasionally used for confinement or as a lookout post.

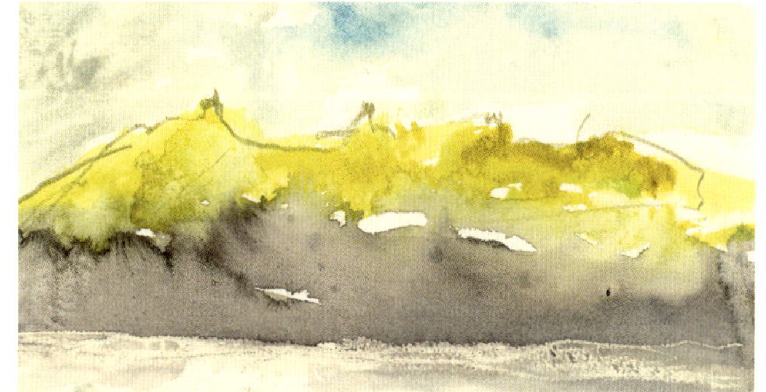

14

The three high points on Papa Little are Second World War gun emplacements guarding the entrance to the bay of Busta Voe. A fishing boat known as the 'Shetland bus' made many journeys to Scandinavia to bring evacuees to Shetland during the Second World War.

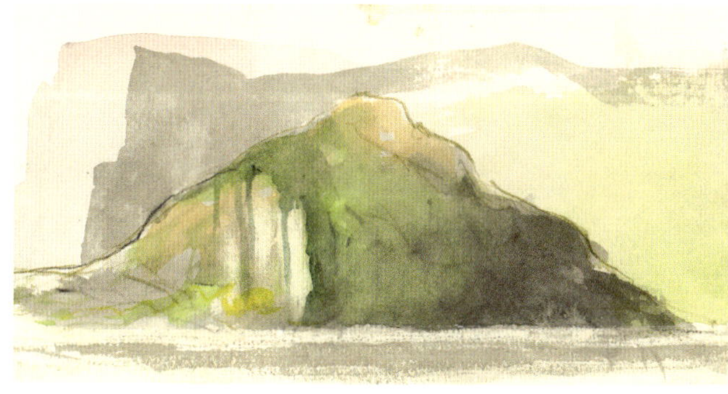

15

The Kame of Foula rises behind Da Noup when seen from the south-west.

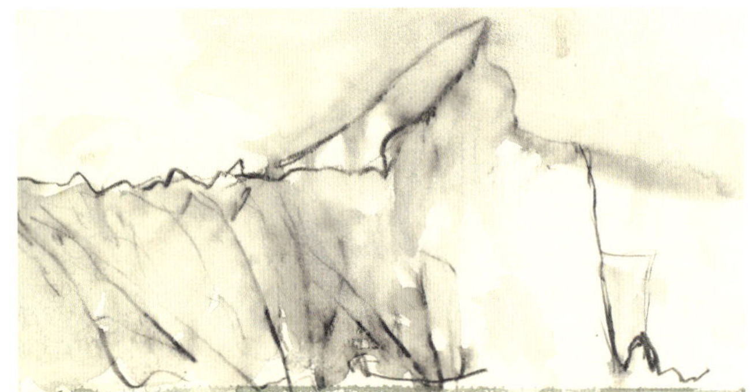

16

In the past, the men of Foula often climbed the sheer cliffs of the Kame as a rite of passage.

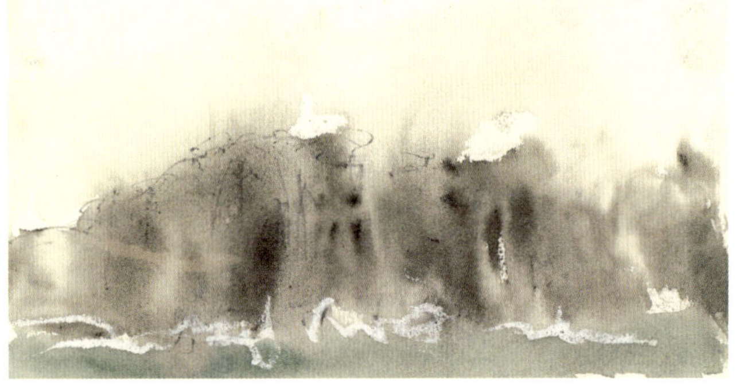

17

The sandstone cliffs of Esha Ness are often shrouded in mist and sea fret as the Gulf Stream finally hits land.

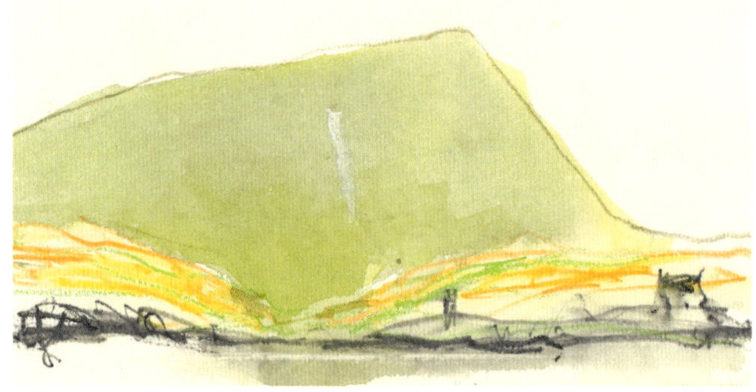

18

The grassy flank of Hamnafield, 344 metres high rises behind the harbour on Foula. A Second World War aircraft crashed just below the summit and fragments of the wreckage can still be found on the grassy eastern slopes.

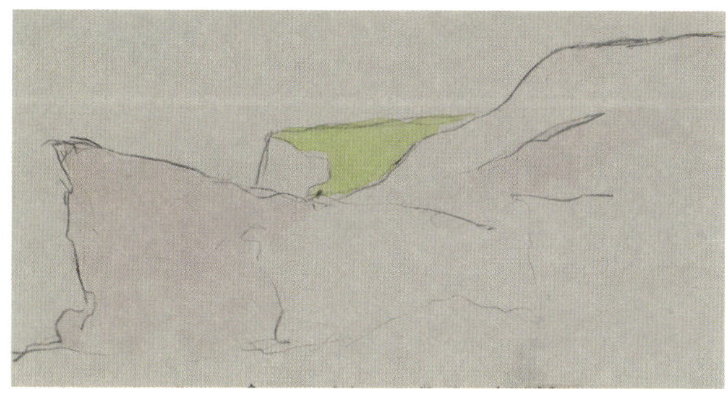

19

Da Sneug is the highest point on Foula.
The Romans could see the peak from Orkney
but never ventured further north.

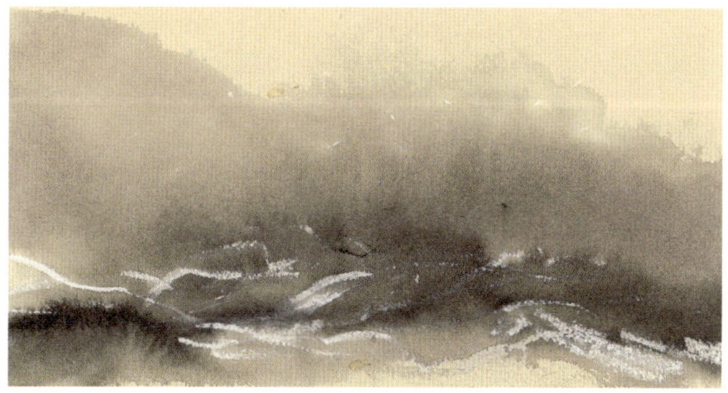

20

Bressay Sound separates the main port
of Lerwick from the islands of Bressay and Noss.
A vehicle ferry makes the short return journey
continuously throughout the day.

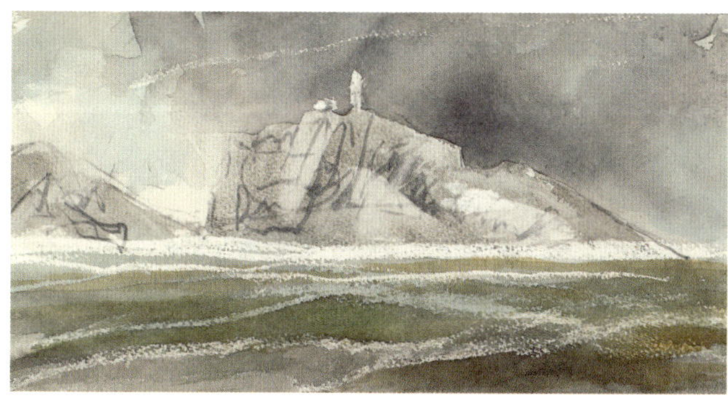

21

Muckle Flugga rock, with its Stevenson
lighthouse, sits off the northernmost point of Unst.
Out Stack and Muckle Flugga are nearer the North
Pole than the southern tip of Greenland.

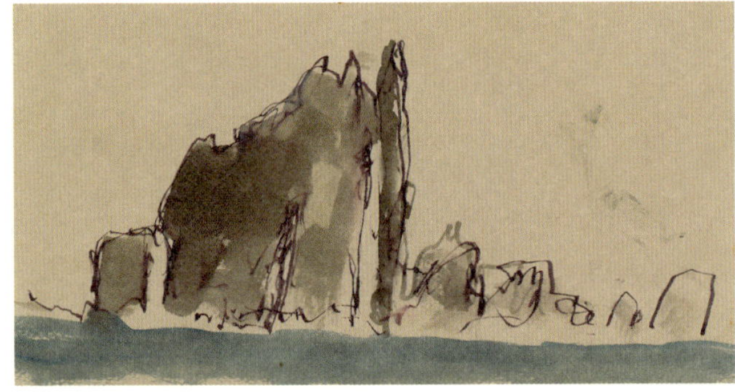

22

The Drongs, off Esha Ness, are here seen from the west with the Ness of Hillswick beyond.

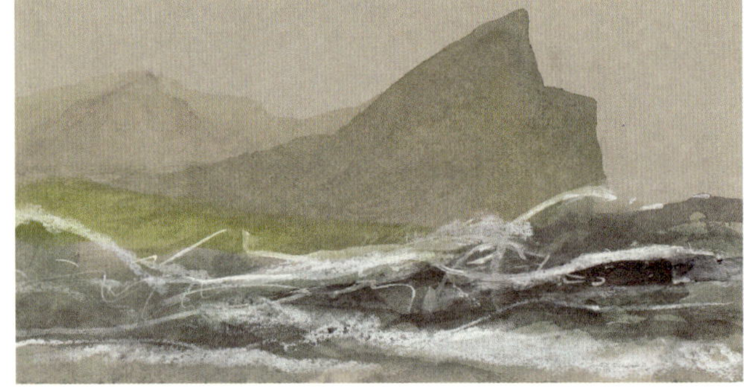

23

From three or four miles away, approaching from the east, the hills and cliffs of Foula echo the swell of the Atlantic.

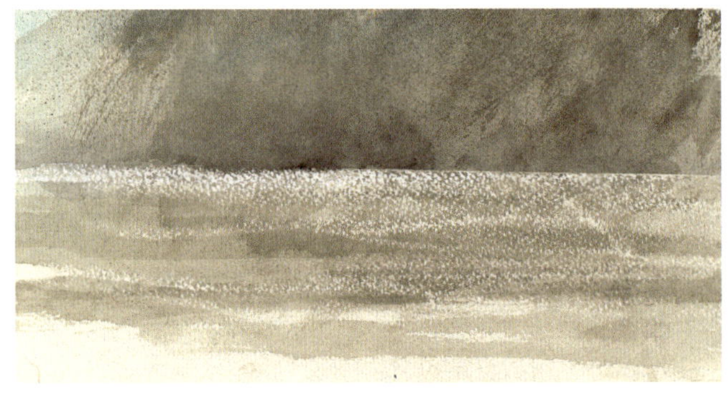

24

Muckle Flugga appears to the west from the entrance to Burra Firth at the extreme north of Unst. Three miles south, deep in the haven of Burra Firth, is the extensive complex originally built to house the lighthouse-keepers' families.

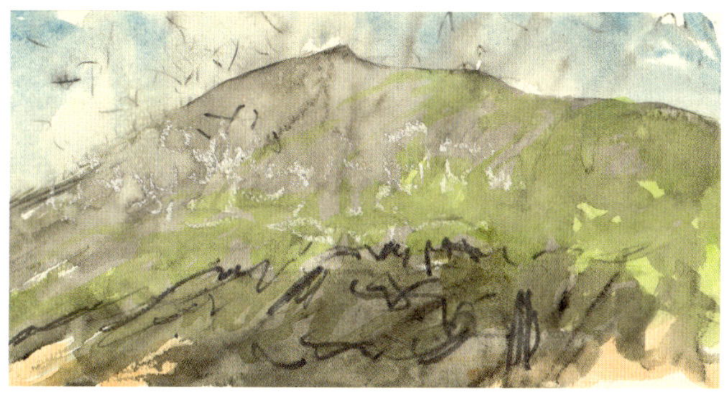

25

The great nature reserve of Herma Ness occupies the entire north-west peninsula of Unst. It is home to enormous and diverse colonies of seabirds – especially great skuas and gannets on the sea rocks and cliffs.

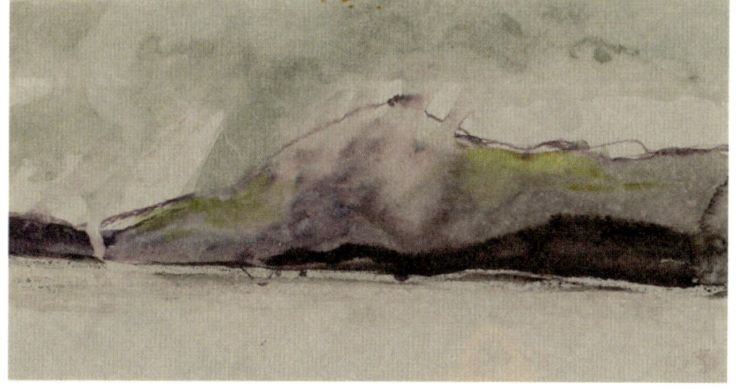

26

Sooth Ness, the most southerly point of Foula, has Da Noup as a backdrop. This is the southern tip of the eastern flatland where the islanders live and grow their crops.

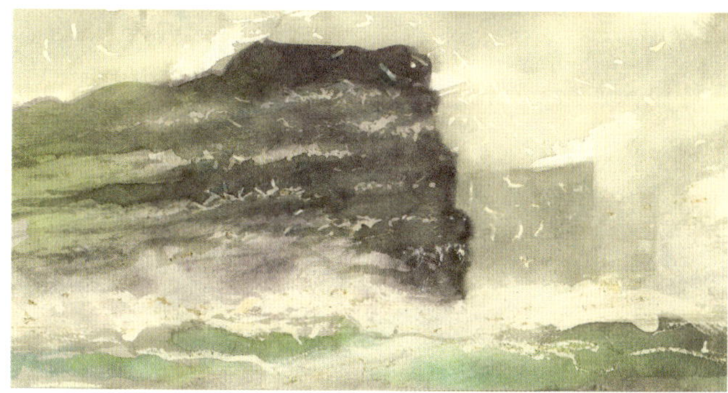

27

The spectacular Rumble Wick and the Noup of Noss can be seen from the Holm of Noss. This is one of the great European seabird sanctuaries.

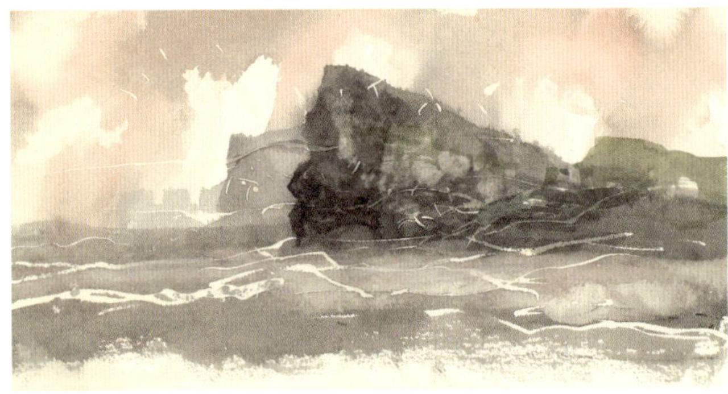

28

Noss Head and the Noup are here seen from the north.

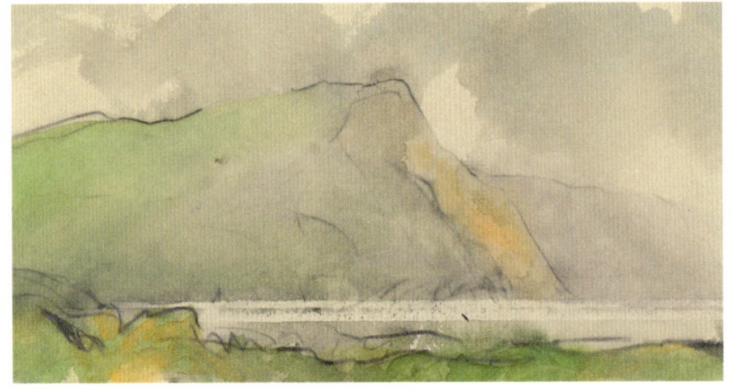

29

The Hill of Setter lies beyond the Noss Sound, seen from Bressay. The whole of Noss is a nature reserve and the eastern cliffs teem with seabirds and skuas or bonxies nesting in the hillside.

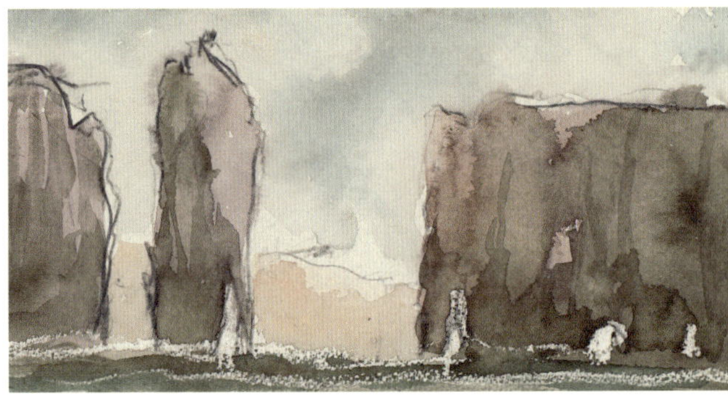

30

The western edge of Papa Stour is carved into fantastic stacks and caves by the Atlantic. The land mass is undercut by the sea into many low channels and tunnels, which can be accessed and explored in a small boat if the sea is very calm.

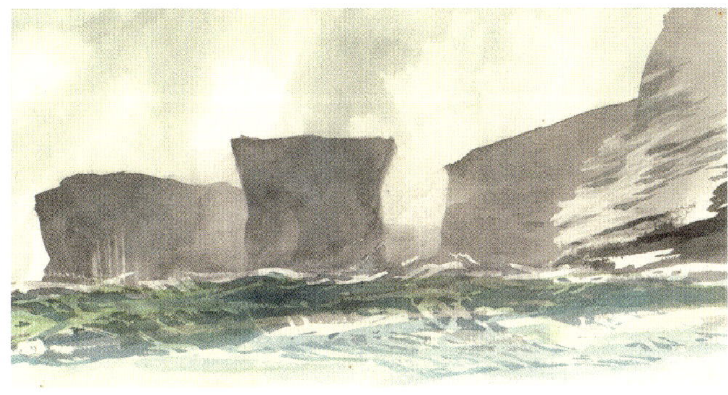

31

The Anvil and the Holm are part of the grotesque group of cliffs and rocks to the south of the east coast of Noss.

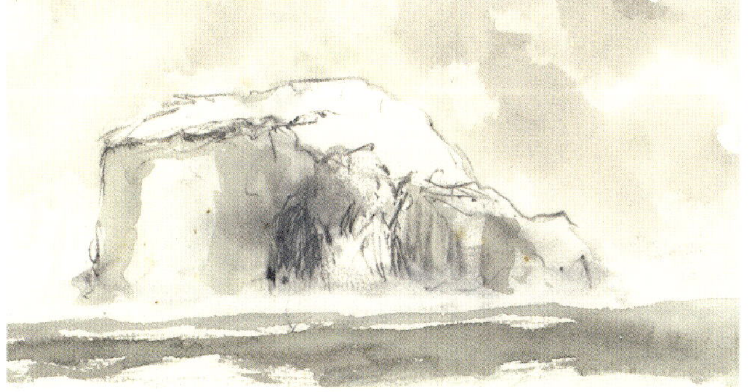

32

Dore Holm, with its precarious and magnificent natural arch, sits in the Atlantic six hundred yards off Esha Ness. In a calm sea one can sail through the cathedral-like arch.

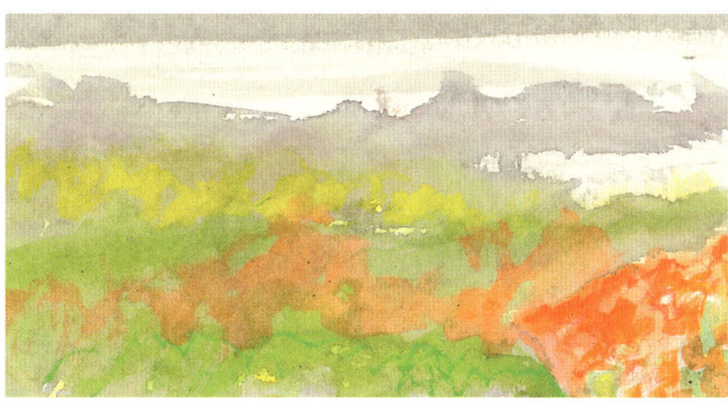

33

In sunlight, especially after rain, the flora on Muckle Roe is rich and pastel-coloured.

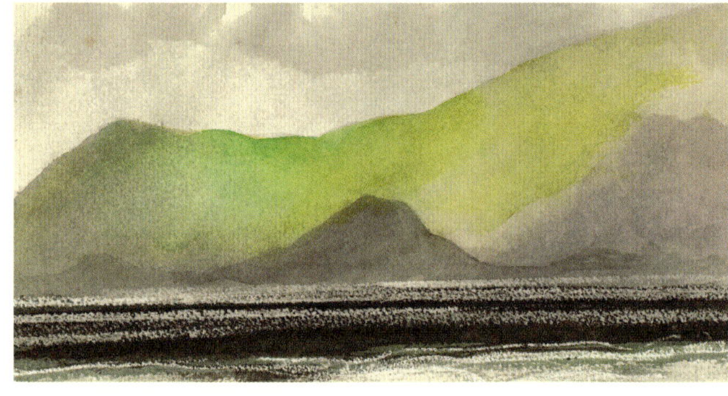

34

The south-west flank of Hamnafield
on Foula is green and rounded.
The flora on Foula in protected low areas
is varied and almost tropical. Orchids and many
other rare species abound.

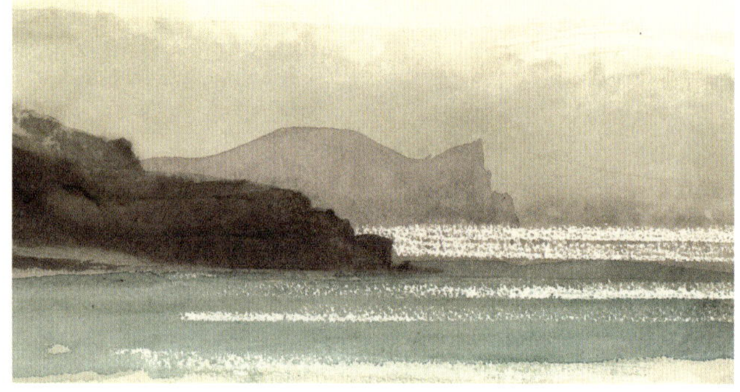

35

From Mainland Shetland, Bard Head on Bressay
and the Noup of Noss can clearly be seen, with the
Sound of Noss dividing them.

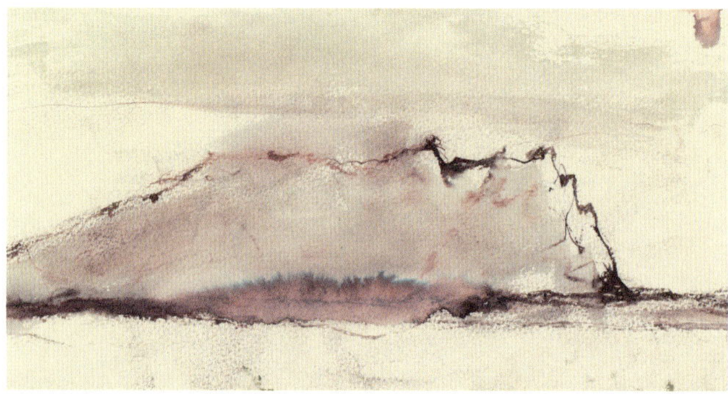

36

Foula is one of the last continuously
inhabited extreme islands in the British archipelago.
Indications of human occupation go back at
least three thousand years.

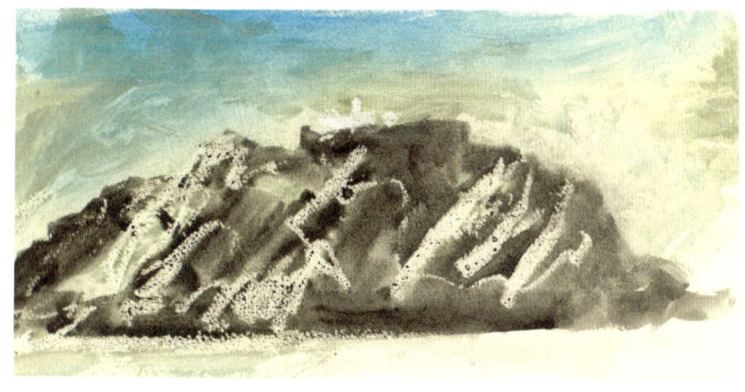

37

The rock strata of Muckle Flugga emerge from the sea at 45 degrees, with many of the ledges home to enormous colonies of seabirds.

38

The protected Brae Wick harbour is to the east of the cliffs of Esha Ness.

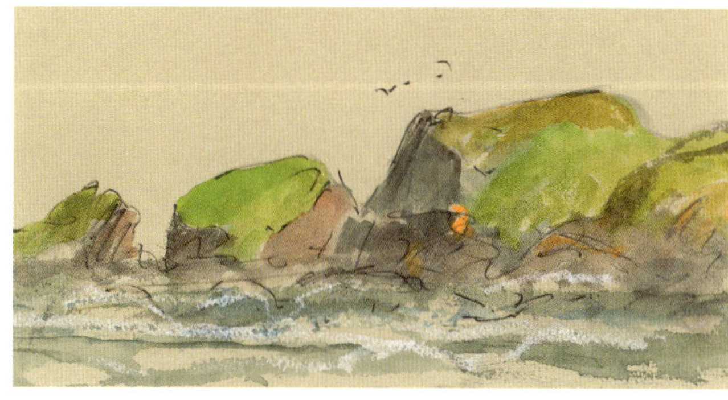

39

The extreme west point of Muckle Roe meets the Atlantic at Strom Ness. The grass-covered knolls and stacks step down into the Atlantic.

British Library
Cataloguing-in-Publication Data
A catalogue record for this book is available from the British Library

ISBN 978-1-907533-89-1:
standard edition

ISBN 978-1-907533-90-7:
limited edition

Distributed outside the United States and Canada by ACC Art Books Ltd, Riverside House, Dock Lane, Melton, Woodbridge, Suffolk IP12 1PE

Distributed in the United States and Canada by ARTBOOK | D.A.P., 155 Sixth Avenue, New York NY 10013

ON THE COVER
The Cliffs of Esha Ness, 2012
Watercolour, 16 × 32 cm

ROYAL ACADEMY PUBLICATIONS
Beatrice Gullström
Alison Hissey
Elizabeth Horne
Carola Krueger
Simon Murphy
Peter Sawbridge
Nick Tite

Book design, typography and cartography:
Isambard Thomas, London

Colour origination and photography:
DawkinsColour, London

Printed in the UK by
Gomer Press Ltd, Wales

ACKNOWLEDGEMENTS
The artist would like to thank:

Edmund Nicolson and his boat the *Julie Rose* for conveying me with good humour to the extremes of Shetland and circumnavigating the Isle of Foula.

George Peterson of Papa Stour for his encyclopedic knowledge of the islands and for arranging a special performance of the Papa Stour Sword Dance.

Felicity Jones for her invaluable assistance during the more frenzied passages of the journey.

Jocelyne and Ian Ritchie and Busta House Hotel for making the evenings so convivial.

The original etching, included in the special edition, was printed on the artist's presses by Niamh Clancy.

LIMITED EDITION
This book is also published in a limited edition of 75 copies, each of which includes *The Noup of Noss* (2014), an etching especially created for this book by Norman Ackroyd CBE RA, printed on Atsushi 67 gsm Japanese paper, and signed and numbered by the artist.